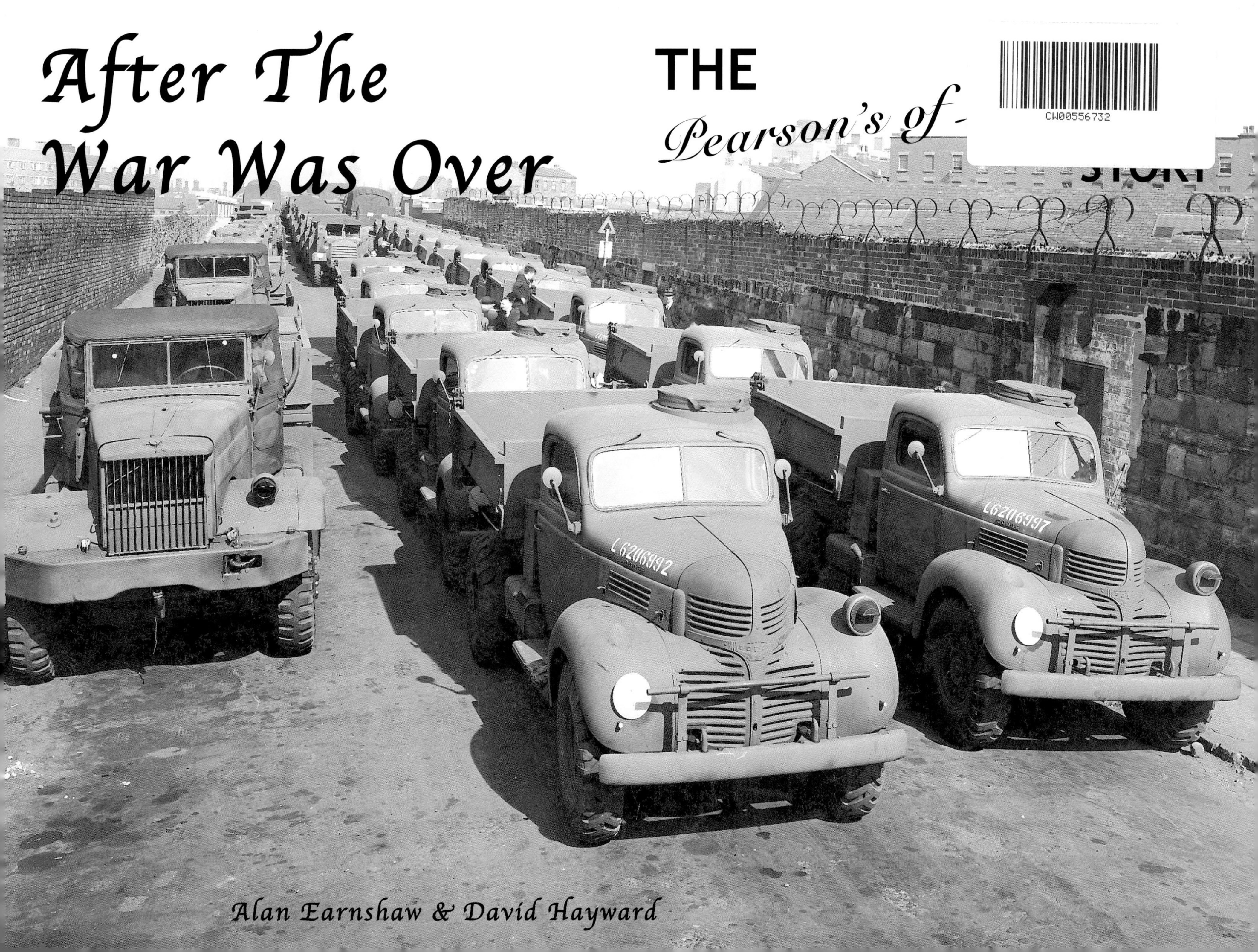

After The War Was Over
THE
Pearson's of
L 6206992
L6206997
Alan Earnshaw & David Hayward

GEORGE JOHNSON & TOM FINLEY

This book owes it existence to the foresight of two men, George Johnson and the late Tom Finley, and it is to them that the authors dedicate their book.

The first of our biographies is that for George Johnson, who was born in Canterbury, Kent in 1918. When World War II started, he joined the Merchant Navy. In 1942 his ship docked in Liverpool and it was there that he met his wife and they married in 1944. When he left the Merchant Navy in 1945 he stayed in Liverpool and became a bus driver for Liverpool Corporation. He later joined a coaching firm called "Sunniways", which was owned by Pearsons of Liverpool who had their showrooms and offices in Shaw Street. In 1950 George went to work for De Havilands Aircraft Factory in Broughton Near Chester. Not only did he work in the factory during the day but he also drove a coach full of workers to and from the Liverpool area to work in the factory. He did this for many years and eventually, he became a Director of "Sunniways" who by now had moved offices to London Road. There he stayed until the Managing Director of "Sunniways" died and the company ceased trading. It was then that the photographs featured in this book were uncovered and George saved them because someone, some day might appreciate seeing them. George Johnson is 90 years of age and resides in a Nursing Home on the Wirral.

It was George's son-in-law Tom Finley, who eventually thought that because of the significance that the subject matter played in 'D Day' and the story behind these photographs, they would be of interest.

Tom Finley was born in Liverpool in 1943. He served his time as a printer in a Liverpool firm. In 1969 he married and moved to work at *The Times and Star* in Workington where he stayed for 17 years. In 1986 he went to work for a printer in Kirkby Lonsdale then moved to Kent Valley Colour Printers in Kendal, where the Nostalgia Road range of road transport books were published. He was always fascinated by the pictures in the books he helped to print, and was extremely encouraging to the Trans-Pennine Publishing team. In his day-to-day life Tom was very happy in his work at Kent Valley and thoroughly enjoyed living in Cumbria. He was always interested in Dad's stories and when the pictures finally came to light Tom was sure that others would also find an interest in them. Tom died in 2003 and he is sadly missed by his family, friends and work colleagues.

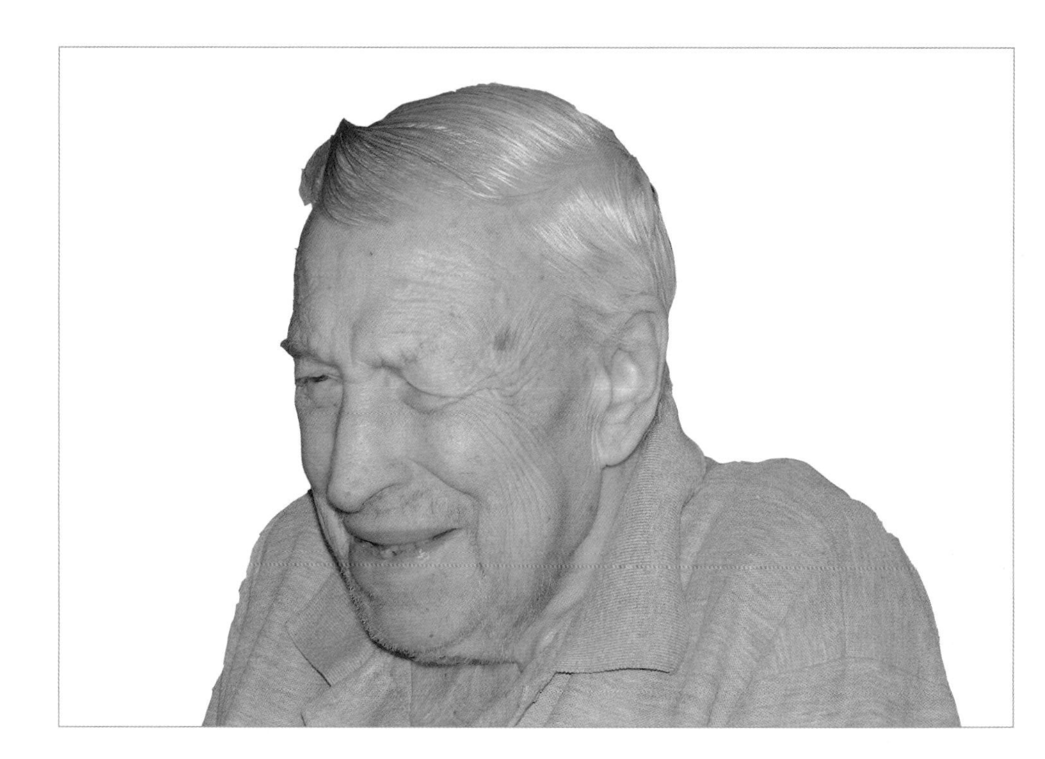

L6206997
L 6206992
After The
War Was Over
THE
Pearson's of Liverpool
STORY

Trans-Pennine Publishing Ltd.
PO Box 10, Appleby-in-Westmorland,
Cumbria, United Kingdom, CA16 6FA
Tel.+44 (0)17683 51053 Fax.+44 (0)17683 53558
e-mail:admin@transpenninepublishing.co.uk
www.transpenninepublishing.co.uk (personal customers)
www.nostalgiaroad.co.uk (trade customers)

printed by
Kent Valley Colour Printers Ltd.
Shap Road Industrial Estate,
Kendal, Cumbria, England LA9 6NZ,
+44 (0)1539 741344

British Cataloguing in Publication Data
A catalogue record for this book is available from the British Library

ISBN 9781903016 28 2 - ALL RIGHTS RESERVED 2008

Pearson's of Liverpool - An Introduction

Over the years I have been involved in the writing, editing or production of well over one hundred and fifty transport books, but I think it is quite safe to say that none of those were as unique as the one now placed in front of you. Its genesis came one day when the then Works Manager at Kent Valley Colour Printers, the late Tom Finley diffidently said: - "Alan, I have some old lorry photographs that my father-in-law George Johnson saved from a garage he once managed after the war in Liverpool; do you think anyone would be interested in seeing them?"

Naturally, without sight of them it was hard to express an opinion, but when Tom brought out a small wooden chest containing the images, he left me speechless, and that (as those of you who know me will testify) is something that is very hard to achieve. Never had I seen such a comprehensive collection of 12" x 10" prints, especially given that they were taken in wartime when normal photography was extremely limited in general conditions, and more so as taking pictures of military vehicles was then not only a criminal offence, but one that carried severe penalties.

Above: *Pearson's of Liverpool, although a long-established business, were really to become a major employer in the years between the two World Wars, especially with the economic rival of the 1930s, when the Mersey ports again bristled with trans-Atlantic trade. A popular song from late-1929,* Happy Days, *epitomised the era. Even the mighty Wurlitzer at Blackpool Tower boomed out the catchy tune, to which holiday makers sang: - "Your cares and troubles are gone, there'll be no more from now on. From now on happy days are here again, The skies above are clear again. So, Let's sing a song of cheer again. Happy days are here again." Several coach companies of the day made much use of the name 'Happy Days', including Pearson's; part of their Happy Days fleet is seen here in 1931, and appropriately all are bound for Blackpool. Of these No.12 even ran an overnight service from Liverpool six days a week. All are Leyland Tiger chassis, mostly TS2 chassis, although No. 4 is a TS1. From left to right are No.8 (KD 9325), No.12 (KF 1267), No.2 (KD 6462), No.4 (KF 3765) and No.7 (KD 9080); most date from 1930, but No.2 is from 1929 and No. 4 from 1931. Number 2 has a Buckingham C32D body, and the rest are said to Burlingham bodies, but there is a view that Nos.7 and 12 may have had Burlingham bodies built under licence by Pearson's workshops. The night coaches had reclining seats, and there were three of these, respectively working from Liverpool to London, Blackpool and Hull.*

However, if you had official clearance, photography was permitted under strict conditions and even then many of the images taken had to have their background 'masked' out, in order to prevent the location being recognised if the picture fell into the 'wrong hands'. Once printed, one set of pictures had to be sent to the Ministry of Supply (MoS), and the other kept in a lockable wooden cabinet; this was the kind of box that Tom had presented to me (along with years of accumulated dust).

I had heard of this 'box' arrangement before, but had never seen evidence of it in over 30-years' research. Yet, it was obvious that those firms who were involved in war-work would have to hold 'photographic record' shots of what they were producing. Many of the images were taken by the Liverpool firm of Stuart Bale, who were paid for the outright copyright; an unusual arrangement under peace-time conditions. The photographers even had to hand over all their glass plate negatives on security grounds.

The images that were retained in the chest had somehow escaped the secrecy and the closure of the wartime factory and then saved from being 'thrown out' as rubbish during the 1950s; they then rested for another half-century in the care of Tom and his family. Not only was their survival remarkable, but so too was their unique subject matter. Most of the images represented the very first example of each type of vehicle to be assembled by Pearson's from the crated vehicles that had been shipped over first from Canada, and then as the war progressed, from the United States of America (USA). Many of the images between 1940 and 1944 show the vehicle's Census Number (military serial number) and my co-author David Hayward has linked these numbers to records that detail the various military contracts.

Several of the vehicles shown here, although not prototypes in the strictest sense of the word, are unique from the models that followed once batch production/assembly commenced. These 'detail differences' are usually very minor in nature, and a classic example is where a photograph has written on the obverse (back) some reference to things, like non-standard wing mirrors and so on.

The book covers a decade of Pearson's history and up to early 1945, when it will be seen that the company's focus was entirely war-oriented and this is clearly reflected in the images we have chosen. However, from around April 1945, the flow of crated vehicles coming across the Atlantic began to slow, as the war in Europe was finally coming to an end, and thereafter the vast majority of output was needed for the war in the East, as Japan was still a major problem to be overcome. From the end of May 1945, the shipments of vehicles that had been shipped across the Atlantic to Liverpool had almost dried up, but Pearson's found themselves extremely busy with the refurbishment of former military vehicles that were needed in the physical and economic reconstruction of Europe.

Not shy of taking opportunities, Pearson's started to purchase the un-assembled and still crated vehicles that were being held in the rurally-located stores they operated for the MoS. They also acquired ex-military units, when these were put into the disposal auctions of the day. Both new and battle-weary vehicles were thus to be found on Pearson's assembly line, where the latter underwent complete refurbishment. This was a time of massive demand for any vehicle, as this had built up during the war years when only a limited supply of new civilian units were available. Furthermore, the post-war restriction on new vehicle production and a concerted export drive by Britain's motor manufacturing industry all fuelled the demand for either new or 'refurbished' vehicles. Again, the photographic record in the box contained significant details of the types of re-built vehicles that Pearson's were then selling to an eager market place.

That record forms the basis for this unique book, as it shows how a relatively minor pre-war vehicle dealer and coach/body-builder not only coped with the war-time conditions, but grew exponentially because of them. The images cover a ten-year period from 1939 to 1949 and the text limits itself to that period, culminating when the firm left their Phoenix Safe Works premises (Liverpool 7) in 1949. They then took advantage of War Compensation to concentrate operations in the more modern factory off Overbury Street, which was located between Angela Street and St. Arnaud Street. At its height Pearson's workforce comprised of 158 male mechanical or engineering staff, 78 carpenters and panel beaters, 44 old age pensioners, 25 boys and 57 women; but cut-backs in the relocation period saw a reduction of over 100 personnel, mostly OAPs, women and a few boys.

We do not concern ourselves with the entire history of Pearson's of Liverpool, its subsidiaries J. Pearson & Sons Ltd, Happy Days Motorways, Sunniways Coaches Ltd, or R. Abram (Coaches) of Southport, nor the car hire, motor agents and the motor mechanic businesses operated by Pearson's Garages of 5-7 Shaw Street, Liverpool 6. The firm appears to have had long roots in Merseyside, as a certain William Pearson was trading as a coach-builder (producing 'fine hansom cabs, Broughams, Cabriolets and commercial vehicles') from a premises called Union Works during the last two decades of the 19th Century. Neither do we concern ourselves with the re-formation of the business as Pearson Brothers Ltd in 1950, nor the sell-off of the subsidiaries and the firm's eventual demise. All these subjects rightly belong in another, completely separate publication. This is merely an over-view of a ten-year span, during which time the firm became a pivotal part of the British and Allied war effort, but nevertheless it is a completely unique record of a time shrouded in mystery and secrecy, which was fortuitously saved by Tom and his family.

Above: *Pearson Brother's head office at Shaw Street in June 1939, where the window displays (from left to right) a Hillman 14, a six-cylinder Morris saloon at £225 and either a Morris 8 or 10-4. Outside is what appears to be a Standard Flying 14, while a 1936 Oldsmobile F36 is standing outside the doors of the Service Department.*

Pearson's Went To War

In common with most engineering firms of any size, during 1938-9, the Government assessed the capacity of the Pearson companies, in order to see what kind of role the firm might play in what looked to be an impending war with Germany. Accordingly, in June 1939, the Pearson Brothers body- and coach-building facilities in an old salt warehouse at 165, Smithdown Lane, Liverpool 7, were turned over to war production for the War Department (WD).

From August 1939, the works came under the Ministry of Supply (MoS), and a number of Ambulance bodies were built for Austin K2/Y and Bedford MW chassis. Ironically, many of the K2/Y 'Katie' ambulances would later be returned to Pearson's for refurbishing after service in North Africa and Italy, to be got ready for the Normandy Invasion. The initial war work included the manufacture of buoyancy tanks for lifeboats, but the Wavertree area around the works was badly damaged during bombing raids in October and November 1940. One of the casualties was Milner's Phoenix Safe Works at the junction of Smithdown Lane and Falkner Street.

Much of the old safe works was completely wrecked, as were the terraced houses on Hope Street. However the ruins provided a 100,000 square foot site on which some of Pearson's activities could be carried out. As for the factory itself, the walls were fortuitously left standing, and this enabled a new roof of asbestos sheeting to be erected. The resulting workshop can be seen on page 71 of this book and this allowed production to be resumed, and before long an 'assembly line' workshop was erected from steel girders and asbestos sheeting (see page 72). The need for these extra assembly line premises followed the bombing of General Motors' Southampton Plant, which had contained the Canadian Mechanization Depot. There was also the associated loss of the firm's military vehicle assembly, civilian vehicle repairing and spare parts facilities.

It was felt that any new assembly facilities would have to be in what the Air Ministry considered to be one of the 'safe' areas of the country, namely where Luftwaffe air-raids were not as prevalent as they would be in the south. Furthermore, by this time Southampton had seen most of its commercial maritime activity moved to the Clyde, Mersey or Bristol Channel ports. As the bulk of the imported vehicles were then being shipped into Liverpool, General Motors (GM) Limited asked Pearson Brothers to see if any suitable premises could be found in rural Lancashire.

As Pearson's had been one of GM's major dealers, they duly obliged and proposed that an old cotton mill Cuerdon [sometimes spelt Cuerden], at Dewhurst Row, Bamber Bridge, near Preston would be ideally placed for receiving the vehicles that were then being imported. Furthermore, the MoS and the Ministry of War Production allowed GM, plus Ford of Dagenham, Essex and Chrysler/Dodge of Kew, Surrey to establish assembly plants located on the River Thames.

In the north, Pearson's were to take full advantage of the situation. Their workshops were the central focus of the operation, despite the bomb damage, temporary repairs and ever-leaking roofs and they remained more or less fully operational, even at the height of the Merseyside blitz.In the following years, Pearson's assembled thousands of 'Completely Knocked Down' (CKD), Semi-Knocked Down (SKD) kits, and Single or Twin Unit Packs (SUP/TUP) from North America; most of which were shipped as crated deck cargo. Liverpool was one of five receiving ports for this kind of traffic, the others being Bristol, Cardiff, Glasgow and Newport. However, Liverpool seems to have been the main centre.

Once the cargo had been off-loaded at Liverpool, it was rapidly shipped out of the city by rail to avoid being destroyed by enemy bombing. These crates were taken to three wooded sites, at Burscough, Ormskirk and one other (as yet) un-identified location, although we are more or less certain that this was just west of the city. At these dumps, a camouflage system was employed to disguise the crated trucks from the air, and from these 'safe' stores the crates would be taken back into the city (two or three at a time) on low loaders. Here the parts would be assembled by a small core of men in 'reserved occupations', who were aided by a number of youths, 'retired' men and an army of women workers. The firm assembled vehicles for the British, Canadian and US forces and [we believe] it also uniquely assembled Jeeps for all three forces.

Bottom Left: *'Happy Days' charabancs seen in the early-1920s; in front is a Leyland G5 or G7, 36hp, 28-seat c1922 and a Leyland-built body. Behind it is a Palladium 28-seater, which carries fleet No.2. It looks to be AK 6823, which was licensed by May 1920 to Douglas & Horner, Bradford, and Leyland expert, Mike Sutcliffe MBE, says that: - "This was still in Bradford in May 1921 either with the same owner or with G. F. Hirst but it had gone from there by 1922 It could therefore have gone to Pearson's. Both are very typical of the era, and the solid tyres would give a uncomfortable ride to the day trippers from the Knotty Ash Brewery, owned by Joseph Jones & Co East Prescot Rd, Liverpool 14.*

Below: *Pearson's Service Van, with the Shaw Street Garage address; it is a Jowett Bradford model, but the vintage is not known but is probably about 1946.*

Above: *This is the Pearson Garage at 3, 5 & 7 Shaw Street, Liverpool 6 in 1938. The black car is a 1938 Oldsmobile F-38 sedan. The cars in the window are 1938 Model Cadet (Kadett) K38 models flanking an Olympia Ol.38; note the emphasis on the 'Products of General Motors Corp'. It was also the office for Pearson's motor coach travel, bureau and car hire service.*

Top Right: *Mind, you car ownership wasn't widespread in Liverpool pre-war, this is traffic congestion looked like in August 1939!*

To these should be added large numbers of British vehicles shipped back for refurbishment and further service under MoS contracts. This included several of the vehicles that were repatriated after the Fall of France, when every truck was worth its weight in gold, due to the high numbers that had to be abandoned by the British Expeditionary Force during the retreat to Dunkirk. Derek Haigh, a fitter at the firm recalled that restoration work went on solidly throughout the summer and autumn of 1940: -

"We were repairing vehicles that would ordinarily have been scrapped, but so great were the shortages at the time, that nothing was ever disposed of." He also recalls that a pre-war OB coach chassis that had been supplied in the summer of 1939 for 'prototype bodywork' was 'frozen' and never completed. He further added that "it gradually began to shrink as various components were removed to repair other Bedford trucks; until only the chassis frame remained." He said that they moved on to the Canadian vehicles acquired for British forces that were assembled, along with some for the Ministry of Food Production and other 'essential civilian users'.

The assembly of vehicles in the UK for Canadian forces, preceded by several months, those supplied by Canada to MoS 'demands' that had been placed in Ottawa in late-June 1940. This also coincided with a huge 'French order', for Canadian and US-sourced vehicles, which were diverted to the UK after the Fall of France; this being some time before the start of the Defence Aid supplies, which in turn were succeeded by the Lend-Lease scheme. By January 1941, the first British-ordered supplies started to arrive.

In Britain, the MoS took over responsibility for all War Department and Air Ministry vehicles (but not the Admiralty orders). They then had to arrange for the vehicles that were not able to be assembled in the new CMD (part of Citröen Cars Ltd, Slough, Buckinghamshire) and Lep Transport Ltd (depot in Chiswick, West London) facilities, which were under direct contract with the Canadian Government.

The Ministry contracted with GM and two other factories for the Chevrolet orders to be assembled for a short time in Bamber Bridge, whilst the Canadian Fords initially went to the Ford Motor Co. at Dagenham, although Ford then set up additional premises. Dodge and Fargo trucks probably went to Kew, but the MoS subsequently contracted numerous companies around the country to assemble both British and Canadian orders from North America. During 1941, on behalf of the Canadian Government, the Ministry appointed various firms to assemble Canadian-pattern vehicles; these being Lep Transport in Goole, Pearson's of Liverpool, Tom Garner Ltd of Pendleton, Manchester, and William Alexander & Sons of Falkirk.

By the summer of 1942, six months after the US entered the war, the assembly of Canadian vehicles reached a low level, because of convoy losses and a resulting lack of components. Consequently, very little assembly was undertaken by any of the 'supply plants', and according to John Bates the younger employees at Pearson's spent quite a lot of time "playing around with Jeeps on land off Smithdown Lane." There was an enquiry about whether these employees should therefore be made available for conscription, but as the supplies of Canadian vehicles was of national importance, the 'reserved occupation' status was 'confirmed'.

A backlog of 'export kits' had built up on the other side of the Atlantic, and this soon reached 10,497 vehicles awaiting shipment from Canada alone. Then, in late-1942, the convoy system became better protected and shipping capacity increased. Consequently, the backlog shifted, but as the kits exceeded the assembly capacity in Britain, the backlog was merely transferred to this country and this required dumps to be set up in Port Talbot and at R.A. Brand & Co. in Manchester to relieve congestion at the assembly plants. This coincided with heavy shipments for the MoS and US forces that were by then being assembled all over the UK as well.

During 1943, the quantities of Canadian Army vehicles required increased, whilst those received from Canada also exceeded expectations. In June 1943, the MoS had agreed a 17% share of total MoS assembly plant capacity, which was supposed to be 17,500 vehicles per month, but the Canadians had more inventory stored than the two other forces. At the same time, crates with US vehicles assembled by the MoS in the TILEFER plants which, like Pearson's assembled British and Canadian vehicles "were piling up at an alarming rate" as assembly fell behind supply. The Canadians stated that lack of suitable labour caused extreme difficulty in maintaining the quality of workmanship and increased productivity.

By August, Citröen and Lep Transport were required to increase output through additional capacity, whilst (from September) Brands were directly-contracted to increase production to 3,000 units per month. However it was felt that, to equip the First Canadian Army for future operations and clear the various huge Canadian crate dumps, 6,000 units per month, needed to be assembled. The answer to this pressing national problem lay with the formation (from 1st October) of 1 CEAU at Bordon, Hampshire; a military assembly operation that achieved in a few weeks 3,000 units per month on top of the civilian output (for instance Pearson's alone made 1,013 in 1942 and 1,866 in 1943). This continued until requirements were met in April 1944, shortly before the Normandy invasion. Subsequently, only replacement vehicles were required and these could be provided from the civilian plants. However, some of these plants also became surplus to requirement, and 30th June 1944 saw Brand's contract cancelled, with similar arrangements made to dispose of surplus stock.

Citröen received the remaining inventory from the CEAU during May and all this material was utilised by the year end. Brands continued to operate a Canadian dump, so material was readily absorbed from there. The US needs were met by establishing Motor Vehicles Assembly or MVA companies, with military personnel at eight depots including possibly an existing one in Wern (Flintshire) and, from January 1944, Bromborough on the Wirral; both were close to the Mersey docks. The MoS also had a heavy reduction in requirements, particularly in the LIEFER programme and they closed a number of their plants in the latter half of 1944.

The US MVA assembly work began to slacken toward the end of 1943, because the most-wanted types were not arriving in sufficient numbers. General Lee, the commanding general of Services of Supply or SOS, directed that the crates that came in were to be sent to MoS plants in order to keep them operating at capacity, even though the US plants were idle. This was because the British plants would be badly needed in the spring when the requirements would bring enormously increased shipments. Most of the seven MVA companies that arrived between January and May 1944 were sent to work in British case dumps near the ports, including Pearson's large dump near Ormskirk, which eventually included US vehicles. By the end of December 1944, Canadian assembly from MoS plants had dropped to 800 units per month: Pearson's contribution being 2,106, bringing the total to 5,834. By 8th May 1945, production had dropped to 400 units per month. By then Citröen reduced their staff and output to 400-500 units per month, with an actual total of 800-900 units per month.

Subsequently CMP assembly was reduced to just six plants, with Citröen operating under direct contract, whilst Pearson's (and five others under MoS contract) were assembling 150 vehicles per week. By 30th June 1945, with requirements finalised, they began running down to a scheduled closure. However, whilst the MoS also faced a big reduction in demand, they had not then finalised requirements and Canadian production ended whilst the plants were still running. The MoS agreed that it was uneconomical to maintain eight storage dumps, some jointly with the Canadians, but Citröen's and Brand's were under direct contract. Consolidation came by the movement of all CMP crates into the dumps at Slough, Manchester and Pearson's, and was completed by 31st October.

The last Canadian-order vehicles assembled by Citröen was on 25th September and Pearson's on 8th October 1945, and whilst a further 5,971 Canadian vehicles were still in the three dumps; Pearson's presumably incorporated British-order vehicles as well. A few 'passenger cars', probably Chevrolet C8A eight-cwt HUP CMPs, continued to be received. Not all of these had been assembled by December 1945 [the last Canadian contract being CDLV 3619], so the MoS arranged for un-crating and assembly in one of their plants in order to keep them going pro-term.

Lep Transport ceased assembly at Chiswick in 1944, and at Goole sometime in 1945. Out of the 33 plants, a total of 88,401 vehicles were assembled by October 1945. The last British orders included Demand S/M 6407 and 6524 for C8A 1C11 Staff Cars (one of the former assembled in Oshawa 31st August 1945), although the plant stopped wartime production around mid-September. There is anecdotal evidence, that the last new vehicles built by Pearson's were a batch of Chevrolet trucks supplied to Malaya in May 1947. During the war years Pearson's assembled a total of 7,737 Canadian vehicles, 1,903 of them in 1945.

The highest known Ford contract was for three-ton F.60L units to Contract S/M 6537, a F60L/WP was built to contract S/M 6537 on 4th September 1945. Yet, as the Auto Workers' Strike started on the 12th, this would seem to indicate roughly when final shipping to the UK commenced. Disposal in the US of surplus military vehicles had started in 1944, being handled by the then War Assets Disposals Board to a market eager for any vehicles. During July and August 1945 the Morrison Mission arrived in the UK to determine what vehicles should be returned to Canada for use by their post-war Army. It ultimately requested that 2,624 cased vehicles were immediately shipped back. A further 3,229 vehicles were held in abeyance, pending a deal with the War Office or other agencies regarding their disposal, and continued to be held until at least November 1945. Of the remaining vehicles, only 169 were found to be surplus to Army requirements and these consisted mostly of tractor units without the cancelled semi-trailers.

By the end of June 1945, some of the crated vehicles had stood in the dumps for as long as three years and a large percentage of the crates needed repairs before they could be moved. With the co-operation of the MoS, the operators of the dumps carried out a case repair programme and all residual cases were made able to withstand a sea voyage by November that year. By then 1,965 vehicles had been shipped, but 659 were held up by a dockers' strike and shipping restrictions. Some vehicles were not disposed of (either in the UK or the Continent), and were donated to organisations and countries for humanitarian work, such as the UNRRA.

Top Right: *Here we have a night scene with the same Hillman and Morris cars as seen on page five, while above the showroom, neon lights pierce the ebony sky recalling reverend Marques of the British Motor manufacturing industry.*

Bottom Right: *A view of the lower (sub-street-level) showroom where, on the far right of the view, a Rover keeps company with more recent Morris saloon cars. Along the top of the window, wonderful period artwork entices 'would-be customers' to enter the premises. Note also the period art-deco railings reflected in the showroom windows.*

Those vehicles and spare parts not reclaimed by the US Government were dealt with at war's end under the 'Settlement for Lend-Lease, Reciprocal Aid, Surplus War Property and Claims', which was effected on 6th December 1945. With regards to Canadian stock, it was dealt with by the 'War Claims Settlement' between the United Kingdom and Canada, concluded on 6th March 1946. The latter agreement settled all claims between the two Governments arising from the disposal in the United Kingdom of surplus war assets of the Government of Canada, or from the disposal in Canada of surplus UK war assets. Therefore, any US- or Canadian-owned vehicles, generators, trailers, etc left in the UK and not claimed by their respective Governments, were then able to be disposed of by the British Government acting through the Ministry of Supply (MoS); most being sold by public auction.

Left: *After the GM Southampton Plant was bombed on 30th November/1st December 1940, General Motors Ltd relocated to Cuerden (or Cuerdon) Mill, near the London Midland & Scottish Railway line outside Preston. These views were taken in the Spring of 1941 at the new GM Bamber Bridge Works. In the background is a No. 12 Cab 1941 Model 8440 Chevrolet Gun Tractor supplied under Demand S/M 2020 (or 2028), [Census Numbers H 4546194 to 4546693; 4593648 to 4594497]. It is chalked up as 'GML1' supposedly being the first vehicle assembled (in the open air) at Bamber Bridge. This official photograph was taken to record a visit to the Cuerdon Mill 'works' by the sub-contract assembly firms, probably after GM Ltd had received MoS contracts. From left to right are Messrs Reginald Cartwright (Managing Director, GM Limited), G. Lloyd-Dixon (Rootes Ltd), C. S. Allanson (Director, GM Limited), R. Pearson of Pearson's Garage, J. Rundbaken (Rootes), H. H. Amos (GM Ltd), and G. Fone of Northern Counties Engineering Company Ltd.*

Top Right: *Here, Mr Pearson is in discussion with Messrs. C. S. Allanson and G. Fone in front of 'GML2'. In the background is a Chevrolet Canadian Military Pattern truck being assembled, probably a C.15 General Service (G/S) truck supplied under S/M 2002 [Census Numbers Z 4440259 to 4443470] or S/M 2016 [Z 4575827 to 4572829].*

Bottom Right: *The photographer records that further discussions were still taking place, at the end of the meeting. Behind the group is a very rare car: a right-hand drive 1939 Lincoln Zephyr V-12 four door Sedan, imported by the Ford Motor Co Ltd subsidiary, Lincoln Cars Limited, Great West Road, Brentford, Middlesex. Lincoln Cars were contracted , as were numerous other companies, to rebuild Ford V-8 military engines during and after the war, as well as undertaking other MoS work, in addition to their usual work and supplies of parts for Ford/Mercury/Lincoln passenger cars.*

Top Left: *The records of Pearson's' photographs did not indicate the position where the images were taken, but we have now successfully established that the company had three assembly plants in Wavertree and Edge Hill. Here we have a February 1945 scene in the upper floors of part of the old Phoenix Safe Works, which shows BSA 500cc M20 motorcycles being disassembled and crated for export (Norton 16H 500cc having also been handled the same way).*

Bottom Left: *This is a much earlier 1941 photograph in the 165, Smithdown Lane premises that for many years had been the operating base for Pearson's Salt Wholesalers. Whether this was a relative of the motor engineering company proprietors is not known, but the authors believe it most likely was. The picture was taken down in the basement, from where ramps connected to the ground floor and thereby enabled supplies to be moved from one level to the next with relative ease. This shot illustrates the huge selection of parts kept by Ministry of Supply contractors. At the time, both GM Bamber Bridge and the Ford Motor Co Ltd in Dagenham had huge stocks of spare parts, which needed to be re-deployed in order to free up space for war production. These parts were thus sold to dealers to keep pre-war vehicles on the road, and of the stocks that remained after the war, most were used by dealers for both refurbished and un-refurbished vehicles. The premises at 165, Smithdown Lane were badly affected in the bombing raids during the period from Autumn 1940 to Spring 1941, and after the massive attack of May 1941 they were almost totally destroyed. According to local sources, and supported by aerial photographs dating from 1945, it has been suggested that little was left of the original Smithdown Lane plant, as just one building was left standing on the site by the time the war ended.*

Right: *For a long time we believed that this view dated from after the war and thought that it showed various lorries that were being re-built and re-painted, whilst on the left on a 'production line' there was an assortment of engines that had been machined and refurbished and then got ready for installation back in the chassis. However, locally provided information has identified this view as being 1942 and taken within the old Phoenix Safe Works after they had been refurbished in the Spring of 1941. This can be determined by the mixture of original stone walls and steel-framed buildings with corrugated asbestos-sheet cladding. One person has suggested that these vehicles had been destined for France, and were actually produced in Liverpool just after the fall of France in May 1941. Quite what has caused the scrape marks down the side of the truck cab on the left is not known, this is a Canadian Dodge half-ton 4x4, whilst the one behind that is a Canadian Military Pattern vehicle with a Number 13 cab and what looks to be a light undercoat in readiness for a 'desert' camouflage paint scheme to be applied.*

H.F.
200
CYCLES

H558
2746

Left & Top Right: *These two views both look down Overbury Street from its junction with Squire Street, and show the old Phoenix Safe Works at the very bottom; note the Windsor Gardens tenements on the right. Lower down on the left is Angela Street, where Pearson's second assembly plant was later erected. This view shows 20 Ford of Canada F60B Bofors, three-ton four-wheel drive Model C39QB tractor CMPs to Demand S/M 2645. These were assembled in 1942-3 and they have had the Census Numbers applied ready for delivery to an issuing depot; the front truck is Census Number H 5582746. There were two Census Number batches, H [for tractors] later S [for 'self propelled mountings'] 5582613 to 5582864 and 6253689 to 6253843. Note the unique open-cab version of the Number 13 Cab, the Number 43S. The gun is a 40mm Bofors. The Willys trailers were popularly known as the 'Ben Hur' trailers and ones seen here would have housed the British-built 'Predictor, AA, No3, Mk1' or 'Kerrison Predictor' by 'M&P Ltd'. The Bofors guns could, in an emergency, be fired from the truck platform without stabilisation and aimed with open 'spider-web' sights, it could even be used when driving at a moderate speed. Normally the truck halted, and the outriggers and jacks were folded out so that the truck-gun platform was secured to the ground; the Predictor was then off-loaded from the G/S trailer and put up on a tripod mount. Thereafter the electrical cables were attached between the Predictor and the gun platform. It is believed that the guns were Canadian-built Bofors rather than the British-built ones by Waygood-Otis.*

Bottom Right: *This location is on the part of Smithdown Lane that is now pedestrianised west of Overbury Street and part of an open park. All of these streets were badly blitzed in 1940-1, as German bombers undertook a series of concentrated raids in an attempt to knock out the vitally important rail tunnels, which in turn would have strangled access to Liverpool Lime Street station and the docks. Although these raids failed to destroy the railways, large areas of housing were destroyed. As a result, the section of Smithdown Lane that ran up to Queensland Street was taken out of public use. Derek Haigh, who joined Pearson's in 1942 (the year this view was taken) recalled that "the bombed out sites around Smithdown Lane and Overbury Street were quickly levelled. The work was done by two Caterpillar bulldozers that Pearson's had assembled, and the land was then used to temporarily store both vehicles and packing crates, but as the threat of bombing subsided this part of Smithdown Lane was turned into a secure compound between the two parts of the Crown Street Railway Goods Yard." He concluded that "this was not so much down to the bombing, but the threat of theft, as unattended vehicles would be stripped of components and have their fuel tanks siphoned dry!" Ultimately, a secure compound was built alongside Smithdown Lane and Grinfield Street. This view shows a one-ton two-wheel Willys G/S Trailer X 5819132, from the batch X 5819091 to X 5819290, and was thus one of several made under Demand S/M 6288. These trailers were used with both the F60B Bofors CMP trucks and Willys Jeeps* *(see also page 67).*

Above: *Although Pearson's stored vehicles in Smithdown Lane, one of their larger stores was to be found along Queensland Street and above Wapping Railway Tunnel. Although the background is censored on this page, the picture to the left identifies this as the location for a view of a soft-top M20 Diamond T 980 or 981, Census Number H 5292491, coupled to a drawbar trailer with a trailer that carries a chalked mark to show Demand S/M 6155, but it should be S/M6156. The 981 was generally described as a 'Recovery Tractor' and was similar to the 980 'Transporter Tractor', but equipped with a 500' rope as against the 300' on the 980's Gar Wood winch. The open cab only saved 136kg in weight, but many were equipped with the American-designed M49 ring-mount for a .50 calibre anti-aircraft gun above the passenger seat.*

Bottom Left: *Another view of the Rogers 24-wheeled 60-ton capacity trailer supplied under Demand S/M 6156. This one appears to have been coupled to various tractors for testing purposes. Order S/M 6156 relates to 12 'Low Trailer 60-ton', delivered on 21st December 1944, but the photographer's record shows that the view was actually taken as early as December 1941.*

Right: *A September 1943 scene shows Diamond T Model 981 Census Number H 5292554, assembled from PKD crates supplied under Demand S/M 2059. This truck was part of the Census batch H 5292229 to 5292728 for 'Tractor 6 x 4 for 40-ton Transporter Trailer'. It was one of 133 Model 981s covered by the US Contract QMC/Defence Aid Contract DA-W-398-QM4 and MoS Demand S/M 2147. Note the cable guide assembly in the front bumper distinguishing the Model 981 from the 980, plus the open cab that was introduced around August 1943.*

H5292554

CAUTION
LEFT HAND
DRIVE
H6164827

Left: *In the Smithdown Lane compound, Diamond T Model 981s and possibly 980s, are pictured in both hard- and open-cabbed versions with their radiator caps removed and radiators drained to avoid frost damage. The trailers are 'Rogers versions' of the British Cranes-designed 'Trailer 40-ton 24-wheel recovery', which in turn were built in the USA by Rogers Brothers, Pointer-Williamette, Winter-Weiss and Fruehauf. The US-built versions had 15" wheels as against the British Cranes 20", hence the distinctive wheel-arch cut-outs and a lower frame. On the right of the street are several 38-ton Allis-Chalmers M6 High Speed Tractors supplied under Demand S/M 6458. The Allis-Chalmers Manufacturing Company was based in Milwaukee, Wisconsin and the M6 (H 6164827) was one of the batch of vehicles H 6164821 to 6164856 'Tractor Tracked for 8"/240mm MG'. If you compare this 1943 view with that shown on page 14 will reveal that the compound wall has finally been completed. The wall to the right of the Allis-Chalmers Tractors has been made from reclaimed bricks from the bomb-damaged house, whilst the concrete wall capping has been studded with broken glass. Careful observation of the page 14 view shows that although barbed wire supports had then been fitted, they were bereft of any wire, presumably due to shortages of that time. That omission has been corrected by the time of this view, and the compound looks reasonably secure.*

Top Right: *This October 1943 view shows a Chrysler (Canada) crated Diamond T 'Medium Breakdown', chassis 969B0325 (403 supplied under Canadian Contract CDLV 587) and TUP Austin K3/YB lorries (to contract BM4799) about to be unpacked in the yard at the back of the Windsor Gardens tenements. Agnes Stubbs (a tenement resident at the time) recalls that children played in and around the packing cases, despite the obvious dangers. She says that they also made plenty of pocket money from collecting the broken packing case pieces and selling these as firewood to the people who lived in the area.*

Bottom Right: *By the time of this view in Smithdown Lane, it was March 1945 and the threat of Luftwaffe attacks on Liverpool had dramatically receded. As the final attack on Germany approached, large concentrations of vehicles built up in the streets near the Pearson's depot and these were protected by a unit of the local Home Guard and Pearson's own night watchmen. Open-cab Diamond T 981s to Demand S/M 2147, stand alongside (amongst other types) Canadian Chevrolet C15TA Model 8449 APC 'Truck 15-cwt 4x4 Personnel' Armoured Truck to Demand S/M 2611 and Canadian Dodge D60S Model T-110-L-6 'Lorry 3-ton 4x2 Tipping' to Demand S/M 6351, Census Numbers L 6206807 to 6207172. To the top left can be seen the Myrtle Gardens tenements on the opposite side of the Crown Street Goods Yard. Built in 1936, this complex of five-storey tenement blocks had originally been equipped with three children's play areas, but at least two of these were taken over by Pearson's and used for the vital war-work, but all work on these sites had ceased by May 1945.*

Top Left: *In this series of official pictures taken of the Allis-Chalmers M6 High-Speed Tractor, we have a record of H 6164827, delivered under Demand S/M 6458. The M6 was arguably one of the most impressive soft-skin vehicles ever built, but the fact that they were assembled by Pearson's at Liverpool has surprised many military historians. This massive 38-ton machine was designed to tow the huge US eight-inch Gun M1 and 240mm Howitzer M1. Note the suspension, especially the exotic idler and the double-width drive sprocket. It will also be noted from the two views on this page, that the M6 had a towing hitch and a pair of 'D' shackles provided fore and aft.*

Bottom Left: *This second view shows the rear detail of the M6. The M6 was a progressive development in heavy High-Speed tractors, and was the next step up from the Allis-Chalmers M4 18-ton High-Speed Gun Tractor, which the US Army used in two variants; Type A carried a rectangular chest at the rear of the hull for 90mm Anti-Aircraft duties, or three-inch Anti-Tank gun ammunition; Type B had a bulged chest with an open top, which could be fitted with different plates for carrying 155mm, 8" or 240mm ammunition and propellant. It was also fitted with a small crane and hoist to handle the loading of the heavy ordnance. As can also be seen, the rear was provided with a heavy duty winch and electrical take-off connector points.*

Right: *Our final official photograph shows the front-three quarters view of the M6 38-ton High Speed Tractor. This was one of the lesser known, but very highly important vehicles used during World War II. Designed by Allis-Chalmers, the M6 looked like an overgrown M4 HST, with a longer wheelbase and wider hull. It was designed to tow either the barrel or carriage sections of both the 240mm Howitzer and the 8" guns, as well as other sectional weapons. While it has often been suggested that the M6 used parts from the M4 medium tank series, it did not; although some parts were common with the M4 High-Speed Gun Tractor. A total of 1,235 were built, it still is among the most elusive of American HSTs to discover. The fact that several M6 HSTs were assembled in Liverpool also came as a surprise to several American military historians, some of whom were disinclined to accept the fact until they saw a copy of the picture on page 18. Those views on this page, which were taken in October 1943, are however more anonymous, as the background details have been obscured by the censors in view of the secrecy that was ruling in the run-up to D-Day. Nevertheless, very careful examination of the things that can be seen tells us that they were taken just beyond the junction of Angela Street and Speakland Street. To help readers orient themselves, had the background of the picture on page 21 not been made opaque, the top left-hand corner would have shown a view of the Overbury Street body-building plant. To put this into context, look again at the picture on page 14, and note the lower of the two public houses (the one displaying Falstaff Ales), and beyond this the second plant was located!*

S/M 6458
H6164827

H5521516

Left: *This January 1944 shot, taken at what was called the 'Gravel Yard' on the partially-cleared area at Grinfield Terrace off Grinfield Street, shows Census Number H 5521516. This is a Studebaker Model US 6x4 'Lorry 10-ton 6x4-2 Articulated' to Demand S/M 2306, part of the batch H 5521384 to 5522208. Demand S/M 2306 also covered 6x4 seven-ton Tractors for semi-trailers, and seven-ton two-wheel semi-trailers, which were used as Low Loading units. Although we cannot be sure, it appears as though Pearson's assembled several Studebakers delivered under the same Demand.*

Top Right: *This Federal 604 'Transporter 20-ton 6x4-4 Semi-trailer' carries Census Number H 4920120 and was thus supplied under Demand S/M 2149. These were originally equipped with the 20-ton Trailmobile Trailers. These tractor-trailer combinations were originally allocated the same Census Numbers, i.e.: the Tractor's number was painted on the trailer, but the trailers were subsequently separated and allocated their own Census Numbers. Similar Trailmobile trailers were assembled by other contractors, such as Lep Transport Ltd in Goole, and towed behind converted Diamond T 980/981 lorries, amongst others. This is a February 1944 photograph and it appears to be the first of those assembled by Pearson's, and as such it was pictured in slightly more prosaic surroundings than the usual cleared bomb sites of Grinfield Street, Overbury Street and Smithdown Lane. This is however the only image we have found taken at Lodge Lane, and it may therefore be unique. To one side of the truck will be seen the Pavilion Theatre, where such music hall 'legends' as Arthur Askey, Gracie Fields and George Formby had all performed before the war. Whether the Pavilion was still open for business at the time of this picture is not known, but it will be seen that the windows are temporarily bricked up. Note the Liverpool Corporation Fordson 7V dropside lorry in the background and John Leary's funeral parlour beyond that.*

Bottom Right: *This is the junction of Smithdown Lane and Queensland Street (with Albert Terrace on the far right. It is not far from the original Pearson plant at 165, Smithdown Lane, which was located on the west side of Smithdown Lane, between Queensland Street and Cardwell Street (northwest of the photographers viewpoint in the photo). The trailer is a 20-ton [US 22½-ton] Trailmobile Trailer Company, and was photographed a week after the Studebaker. The trailers were to the same Contract Demand S/M 2149 as the Federal 604 tractors to which this one seems to have been attached, and were allocated X 5847938 to 5848387. However 'Trailer 20-ton 8-wheel (4 twin)' was listed by 1944 as 'Separated from Contract S/M 2149'. Much of this area was damaged on Saturday 3rd May 1941, when Liverpool faced the most harrowing night in its 800-year history. It was estimated that up to 500 German bombers were involved in the bombing of the city, which lasted from 10.30pm to 5am the next morning, though the defenders shot down 16 planes that night, the damage to the city was appaling.*

Top and Bottom Left: *Although censored, these pictures were taken in Oliver Street near St. Nathaniel's Church and shows a Mack LPSW dump truck produced by the Mack Machinery Corporation. It is experimentally coupled to a 60-ton Rogers trailer, presumably that seen on page 16. This kind of trailer was used mainly to transport heavy engineering equipment, but is nevertheless unique, especially given that it was not known that this combination was ever produced/assembled in Liverpool. Other firms are more commonly associated with the assembly of these dump trucks, notably Lep Transport at Goole.*

Below and Right: *Produced for the American army by the Autocar Co of Ardmore, Pennsylvania, this was a 'Tractor 4x4 for Mobile Oxygen'. It was later acquired by the Ministry of Supply under Demand S/M 6406 in the batch H 5877462 to 5877475. This one still has its previous USA registration number USA56513S and S/M 6406 chalked on the left side. Derek Haigh, a former fitter at Pearson's states that this was probably the model that was shipped from America to Avonmouth and was driven up from the Bristol Channel port in 1942 by a fitter called David Turner. He recalls that: "Pearson's were not really concerned with assembling these tractor units, but they did build the Oxygen-Nitrogen Generating trailers that were coupled to them and that this unit was supplied for draw-bar testing"; if so it would explain the rather work-worn condition in which it appears in these pictures.*

USA

Mack

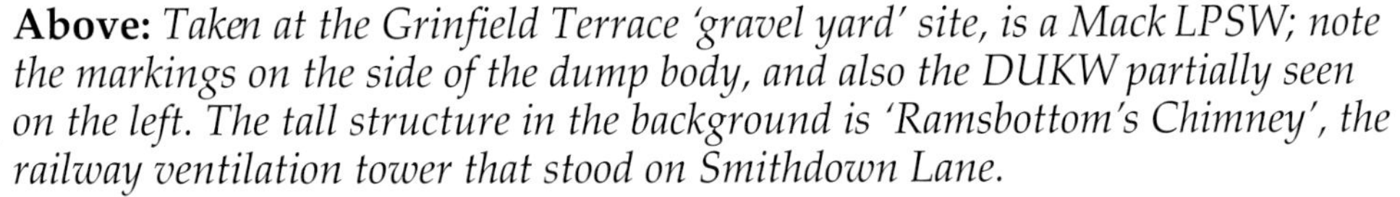

Above: *Taken at the Grinfield Terrace 'gravel yard' site, is a Mack LPSW; note the markings on the side of the dump body, and also the DUKW partially seen on the left. The tall structure in the background is 'Ramsbottom's Chimney', the railway ventilation tower that stood on Smithdown Lane.*

Left: *An October 1942 view in Smithdown Lane, taken where the street climbed towards the railway bridge. The Mack LPSW was a 6x4 17½-ton Dump Truck, which had a 160bhp Thermodyne petrol engine, and had been acquired under Demand S/M 6132. These had military features, although may have been acquired by the MoS for the Ministry of Works. The rear-tipping body held 12 cubic-yards; this had a hoist underneath and to the front of the engine and cab protector. Behind the Mack is a Dyson 20-ton trailer, and what appears to be several FWD HAR-1 Sno-Gos. On the right side of the street are some Ford GPWs (Jeeps); on the left the Myrtle Gardens complex can be seen over the wall.*

Top and Bottom Right: *In two views we see the impressive size of the Mack LPSW. This is emphasised by the opaque background on this 'de-sensitised' photograph. The uncensored image, taken in Overbury Street, with the LMS railway warehouse in the background, draws a contrast in size between the LPSW posed adjacent to a US-order Ford GPW Jeep, assembled by Pearson's to a US contract, but they also built Jeeps to Canadian and British contracts.*

H5854373
S/M 6175

Left: *Here we have a selection of photographs taken on Crown Street in low spring sunlight during 1942. This lorry, which had just been assembled by Pearson's has just had its WD Census Number (H 5854373) applied, identifying it as a 15/16-ton 4x4 FWD model SU-COE tractor. The manufacturer of these models had factories in Clintonville, Wisconsin, plus another in Kitchener, Ontario that was known as The Four Wheel Drive Auto Company Ltd. This latter plant supplied the Canadian and British orders with Canadian bodies added to chassis-cabs railed from Clintonville. The Kitchener factory then crated up dis-assembled FWD trucks (and also Jeeps and other vehicles) for shipment to the UK for assembly. During World War II, the Ministry of Supply ordered militarised versions of the FWD H- and U-series, the latter mainly the Cab-over-Engine of the SU, the militarised SU-COE. The engine was a 517 cubic in six-cylinder Waukesha SRKR, driving through a five-speed transmission to a permanent four-wheel drive. There was a lockable third differential in the transfer case, so that maximum traction was obtained at all times without wind-up in the drive line.*

Top Right: *This shows the official near-side view though with just a hand-written Demand 'S/M 6175'. The two prop-shafts and the transfer case can be clearly seen. It also shows a good side elevation of the bodywork, which was similar to that used on the AEC Matador artillery prime mover. The MoS Record Card for Demand S/M 6175 shows that it was issued in 1943, initially for 3,000 'Tractor 4x4 Heavy SU' for delivery from the US factory, but the amount has been crossed out and later '500' corrected. Census Numbers H 5834373 to 5854522 were allocated, with 'L' for 'Lorry' replacing the 'H' for 'Tractor' prefixes on 6th October 1944. Delivery was intended initially for the UK, but this then appears to have changed on 21st April 1944 to 176 for the UK and 350 for India, at which time 'Medium' was substituted for 'Heavy'. The description then looks to have been changed again by a hand-written notation on 6th October 1944, this time to 'Lorry 5/6 ton 4x4 G/S'. As the face of the war in Europe was then changing, obsolete gun tractors and portees were soon being re-built to G/S vehicles. Note the sole left-hand headlamp with brush guard, and towing rings on the substantial flat-section bumper. These views show that the stencilled number has not been applied to the near-side door.*

Bottom Right: *This rear three-quarter view shows the body raised up well above the rear axle. It will be seen that the towing hook was originally fitted as part of the spare wheel carrier, whilst the stencilled Census Number is painted on the right of the tailgate. The body has the usual hoops with a tarpaulin covering.*

Top and Bottom Left: *This series of views on these two pages allow us to make some interesting comparisons in the two makes of Canadian Military Pattern vehicles (Chevrolet and Ford). On the left we see a front-three-quarter and a rear-three-quarter view of a 1943 Ford Model C298QF F60L, with a No.13 type cab. This one is shown carrying Census Number L 5827892, which is for 'Lorry 3-ton 4x4 Workshop' to Demand S/M 6178, and this is also seen chalked on the door of what was probably the first of the ones to be assembled by Pearson's. There were two batches L 5827691 to 5827980 and L 5836461 to 5836689. Note the short-neck gas tank filler pipe, and the application of the Census Number. This has been stencilled on the door, although it has not been painted on the other side at the time of the photograph.*

Above and Right: *Two views of a General Motors of Canada version, a 158" wheelbase Chevrolet Model 8443, which was described as a 'Lorry Three ton 4x4 G/S', more commonly known as a C60L with No.13 cab and all-steel General Service (G/S body) with canvas canopy. The side curtains are of the three-panel type as against the four-panel type design used later. This was probably a '1943 Model' delivered under Demand S/M 6110, Census Numbers L 5429530 to 5432050, as it was photographed that October. The truck on the right is a similar model; note the square roof hatch, the location of the spare tyre and the long version of the gas tank filler pipe. It was supplied under S/M 2691.*

W/T

Above: *The CMP assembly at Pearson's also included armoured vehicles, although this has not hitherto been widely appreciated. In the pictures on these pages we show different models photographed in Sefton Park, close to the assembly plant. The view above is apparently the GM of Canada Chevrolet C15TA 4x4 101" whælbase 'pilot' Model 8449 APT 'Truck 15-cwt 4x4 Personnel' Armoured Truck; one of three initial trucks sent CKD to Liverpool for assembly at the end of 1943. The hulls were fabricated by the Hamilton Bridge Company, where 3,961 were produced. Note the 10.50 x 16 tyres and wheel hubs with flanges for slings, and the 'O' painted on the front sides.*

Top and Bottom Right: *The Canadian designation for this model was C15TA-ARMD-1 and the MoS ordered these trucks together with the wireless and ambulance versions to Demand S/M 2611. The model had the canvas cover at the rear, and the lower view shows the tarpaulin buttoned back with the armoured door pegged open for easy access. The view also shows the details of the driver's and commander's positions, the six personnel seats, the wire stowage baskets and the rifle clips. Note the external storage bins that doubled as wheel arches and rear fenders while the two brackets on the outside of the body are protectors for the tail lights that also serve as steps. At the front, the driver's station shows that the controls are basic and to the later CMP pattern. The truck has removable floor plates that would open up to reveal foot-wells for the seats that were bolted to the checker-plate steel flooring.*

Left: *The truck seen here is the second version of the Chevrolet C15TA, this time however it is an Armoured Wireless Car C15TA-ARMD-1WT, as noted by the 'W/T' painted on the front sides. It is again seen in Sefton Park, although in the Spring of 1942. This version of the C15TA has a two-piece cover with transparent panels allowing the back portion of the body to be open, while the front end provided cover for the commander, driver and wireless operator. Note the gun ports to the side of the two front windows.*

Top Left: *This view, looking east up Smithdown Lane from its junction with Overbury Street, has been included here because it shows (in part) two International Harvester M14s (from the batch Z 6111136 to6111184). These were known as 'Truck 15-cwt Half Tracked Personnel' trucks and supplied to Demand S/M 2176 in the batch Z 6110575 to 6111574. In total, there were eight Census Number batches covered by three Demands (S/M 6105/6173/6176), the first four being listed as just 'Truck 15-cwt Half Tracked'. Pearson's later refurbished trucks similar to those shown here that they acquired from the MoS in the post-war disposal sales. The Pearson factory in the old Phoenix Safe Works can just be seen in the top right-hand corner.*

Bottom Left: *This is an official photograph of a Caterpillar 'Tractor D8 Diesel' produced by the famous Caterpillar Tractor Company of Decatur, Illinois. It was found in the Pearson files and had been printed out in a transposed (back to front) view from a negative. Writing on the envelope that originally contained this image suggests that it was the "only one produced, subsequent supplies lost at sea due to enemy action." This may well make this one unique, as only a maximum of 30 were known to have been built to a British military order. These, in turn, were supplied under Demand T724, and allocated Census Numbers H 4473862 to 4473891. Substantial numbers of D8s were shipped by the US Army direct to Europe as ready-assembled, but several CKD versions were also sent via the huge US military supply depot at Micheldever, Hampshire, which was better known as 'Woolworths'.*

Right: *According to the Census List, the vehicle seen here (Z 5874161) was a Bombardier 'Truck 15-cwt Tracked G/S', to Demand S/M 6028 and was part of quite a large batch running from Z 5874161 to 5874541. Obviously, the pioneer in the 380-strong class was assembled at Pearson's, but this is the sole photographic reference to such a vehicle in the entire collection, so whether the Liverpool company made any others is not known. Furthermore, the Census Book description is a misnomer, as it was in fact an Armoured Snowmobile. Its technical description was: Snowmobile, Canadian, Armoured MKI (Farland & Delorme) with a 125-bhp Cadillac V8-cylinder, and a 4F1R (Hydramatic) gearbox, but it was also known as 'Car, Armoured, Tracked'. Its role was as a Light Reconnaissance car with a crew of two, a No.19 W/T set, Bren and Sten gun etc., 16" Run Flat tyres (4.50-16) and 35" tracks. The V8 petrol engine drove the front sprockets through the four-speed automatic transmission and a Ford T16 Universal carrier axle with controlled differential steering. In the spring of 1943 the MoS had expressed an immediate requirement for a two-man reconnaissance snowmobile, but production was only started in spring 1944 by L'Auto-Neige Bombardier at the Farland & Delorme factory in Montreal.*

S/M
6028
Z.5874161

Above and Bottom Left: *Storage of the CKD crates could not be concentrated in the city, especially the dock areas, for fear of enemy bombing raids. Indeed, a memo from Admiral Raeder, to Adolf Hitler in May 1941, urged the Fuhrer "That an early concentrated attack on Britain was necessary, on Liverpool for example, so that the whole nation will feel the effects." As a consequence, dumps were established in Liverpool's Wavertree and Sefton parks, but although these crates were well camouflaged, they were still vulnerable to accidental damage in 'tip and run' air-raids. Three larger dumps were then established outside the city, the largest of which was outside Ormskirk; we cannot say for a certainty that this is that larger dump, but it is certainly quite a size! Note that at least ten cranes, both fixed and mobile (some hired from George Cohen) are visible, as is a circular static water tank and pre-fab housing for the workers.*

Right: *This appears to be Mr R. Pearson with a US Army officer at the same dump, on an inspection tour of US-owned vehicles assembled under contract apparently in late summer 1944. The car is a 1939-41 Humber Snipe or Super Snipe with its identity subsequently 'censored'; however by judicious use of modern photograph manipulation software, the serial number USA 1823774 can be made out on the bonnet although this is only just visible in this view.*

COHEN
HUMBER

Left: *Another of the stunning pictures from the collection, this view shows one of the crate-handling facilities adjacent to the Pearson factories. This is located on the patch of land between the Phoenix Safe Works and the block of tenements called Windsor Gardens. These tenements were a 'U-shaped' complex that had its opposite leg on Oliver Street, and had been built on the site of cleared houses on Harding Street, Swan Street, Corlett Street, Linden Street and Roger Street. It was built in the 1930s and access to the flats was via prominent stair towers on the outside and balconies at each level. In the background, the row of earlier tenements on Albert Terrace can be made out across the Crown Street Goods Yard. This view dates from 25th August 1944, when it was (apparently) relatively safe from the Luftwaffe, and it shows several soft-cab 2½-ton 6x6 GMC CCKW-353 lorries. These look to have been made to an American-order, with wood stake bodies; several of which have longitudinal slatted seats in the back. We also see a damaged CMP No 13 cab, as well as a 6x6 heavy mobile crane that has been pressed into 'depot' service by Pearson's staff. On the rest of the former playground site, mountains of crates can be seen; several of them stencilled Chrysler, Dodge and WLF/Ward La France!*

Top Right: *This picture shows the Sidney Gardens Tenements on Sidney Place, with Grinfield Street seen at right angles in the background. The image is dated 8th February 1944 and shows GMC 'Amphibian 2½-ton 6x6 G/S' Model DUKW-353 or 'Ducks', to MoS Demand S/M 2849, posed for the camera. They were equipped with a GMC 270 cubic-in six-cylinder engine similar to the CCKW-353, with which it shared a 164" wheelbase. There were several Census Number batches for these amphibians, including P 5216042 to 5216218, P 5477051 to 5477350, P 5544759 to 5544958, P 5575591 to 5576590 and P 5815051 to 5816050. The front vehicle seen here is P 5576524 and the convoy of four are awaiting to re-enter the Pearson's works for modifications after their acceptance trials at Ainsdale near Southport.*

Bottom Right: *This view dates from March 1944 and is also taken on the triangular site between the former Blucher Street, Grinfield Street and Smithdown Lane. It shows several 10-ton 'Tractor 6x6 Break Down Heavy', which were made by either the K. W. Kenworth Motor Truck Corporation of Seattle, Washington or the Ward La France Truck Corporation of Elmira Heights, New York. These are more likely the latter, but both were described as being M1A1 181" wheelbase models with Gar Wood cranes. There were several batches to Demands S/M 2342; S/M 2525; S/M 2660 and finally several that came from US forces. In the absence of any Census or Demand numbers, it is not possible to say which these are, but it is likely that they were newly assembled and awaiting numbering outside Sidney Gardens.*

Top Left: *After being transported from the docks or the storage dumps by road or rail, the crates were unpacked at one of three sites around Pearson's factories. Most of the crates were then flattened and many were re-used, whilst the damaged ones were chopped up for firewood by enterprising children from the locality. However, some empty crates were stored, like these seen dumped around the back of Myrtle Gardens in March 1945. The stencilling indicates that the slightly battered one in the front had contained a Mack Machinery Corporation '6 ton Prime Mover Model NM' (NM5 'Heavy Artillery Tractor' but by then assembled as a six-ton load carrier). The serial number was USA 539247, and this was supplied under Contracts W2425-QM-710 and W-670-ORD-3352 (Demand S/M 2311 of 19th November 1941) and crated '11/30/43'.*

Bottom Left: *This is another of the official pictures taken by Stuart Bale photographers for Pearson's and the official records, and is captioned '7½-ton Mack S/M6242'. This time it shows a Model No.6 built in Allentown or East Allentown, Pennsylvania and supplied under Demand S/M 6242. Census Numbers allocated were H 5589005 – 5589104 and 5837426 – 5837549, for 'Tractors 6x6 Super Heavy'. This vehicle has a wooden body and Gar Wood 5 MB winch and was intended to tow the 155mm gun, but when photographed had evidently been converted to a load carrier as the Census Number has an 'L' prefix before '5559024', which may have been a mis-stencilling for '5589024'. Note 'CAUTION LEFT HAND DRIVE' on the rear. This view is looking north from the triangular 'gravel yard' site towards Grinfield Street, just opposite its junction with Mason Street.*

Right: *This view is looking north from the site of Grinfield Terrace on the 'gravel yard' site, just to the east of the Bay Horse Hotel. The first building visible beyond the corrugated iron fence is 19, Grinfield Street, the end terrace of a block of nine houses and a shop. The building beyond No. 19, to the left of the tramway stanchions, is 16, Congress Street and beyond that is 15, Congress Street. The building behind the rear of the truck, with the semi-circular bay and railings is the Wine & Spirits Vault on the south-west corner of Grinfield Street and Mason Street. Few people today will remember what the area was like before it was blitzed, but John Bates of Garstang, Liverpool, vividly recalled the 'Gravel Yard' when talking on the BBC, saying: - "Jeeps, GMCs, Macks, Dodges; they all came in on the convoys that were getting through from the States. All were packed in crates and had to be put together, it was great. When the convoys were getting sunk and no crates arrived, the big gravel store yard [being empty] was ideal for racing round in the four-wheel drive Jeeps. The handbrake on a Jeep was on the dashboard which was pulled out to stop, and hitting it down would release the brakes. So we would head towards the fence, then jam it in reverse, let the clutch out and hit the brake off, skidding to the fence with the wheels going backwards and seeing how close we could get to it."*

DANGER
400 VOLTS

F251
BEDFORD
TROOP
CARRIER
BEDFORD

Left: *On 12th September 1939, Vauxhall Motors were given the go-ahead to develop a three-ton 4x4 military lorry and despite all their other commitments by 1st February 1940, an experimental forward-control QL model was undergoing road trials, followed by two more a month later. The engine chosen was the standard six-cylinder 28hp Bedford of approximately 3.5-litres, similar in size and design to that of the Canadian Chevrolet 216 cubic inch six-cylinder. The drive went via a Bedford gearbox to the front and rear axles through a transfer case, which was similar to Chevrolet and Ford CMP designs. The driver would normally use two-rear wheel drive, but they could engage a lever on the transfer case to engage the front wheel if required. The MoS subsequently placed substantial orders for production lorries from 1941 for the Army and RAF, and for non-military use in other Government Ministries. The Admiralty also placed orders for the Royal Navy. Thus the QL became the fourth type of 'WD' vehicle to go into production. Although the MoS also contracted Ford to produce a similar three-tonner, the W0T6 (and 30-cwt W0T8), the QL was by far the most numerous three-tonner 4x4 in service with a production run of 52,245. Various QL models were produced; including the model QLB Tractor unit for Bofors 40mm AA gun, the QLC Semi-trailer with a six-ton capacity and soft-cab six-pounder Portee, the QLD Standard Covered Wagon (multi use), the QLR Wireless/Telegraphy, the QLT Troop Carrier (seen here) and QLW Tipper lorry with winch. This photograph and the following one are dated November 1944, and show the then-current camouflage scheme created by three blasts from a spray gun with the nozzle at its widest setting. Bedford held their favoured position with the Army until the early 1990s, with their range of subsequent four-wheel-drive military trucks, some of which are still in service.*

Top Right: *The Census Number L 560479 identifies it as one of the batch L 559110 – 562075 supplied under Contract V.4914, for 'Lorry three-ton Troop Carrying and W/T', and V.4924 for 'three-ton Troop Carrying'. Allun Armstrong, a former Pearson's worker recalled that: - "Large numbers of QL Troop Carriers were sent to Africa and later the Far East, having been delivered from Luton as chassis cabs. Pearson's then produced the Austin-type bodies, which were then knocked down and stored on the back of the chassis frames and sent for shipping." Note also the 'LOT 521' chalked on the cab as well as 'F 251', '260' and 'BEDFORD TROOP CARRIER' on the body, which are thought to be for the shipping manifest.*

Bottom Right: *The prototype QL is being tested at Luton Hoo in 1940, with a different radiator grille to the production model that we have seen in the two previous views. The Bedfordshire trade plate was used only for road trials and this particular 'test' vehicle was never handed over to the War Office. Vauxhall Motors came up with various 'solutions' for these models during the war, including waterproofing to enable 'amphibian' landings on D-Day.*

Top Left and Right: *These two photographs are taken at a location not seen in any of the other views within the Pearson collection. Again, the surrounding vehicles all have evidence of significant bomb damage. This view is actually looking south towards Upper Parliament Street along Oliver Street from its junction with Faulkner Street. The large building on the right of the photograph is the Windsor Sugar Mills, whilst the west wing of Windsor Gardens is just out of shot to the left. The small section of building just visible on the left of the photograph is St Nathaniel's Church on Pine Grove. The buildings in the distance on the right of Oliver Street run from its junction with Pine Grove to its junction, in the far distance, with Upper Parliament Street where a large public house stands on the corner. The sugar mill still stands, and is now part of Renshaw factory, which today makes marzipan and other confectionery items. The two views show a convoy that is presumably about to be delivered to an issuing depot in May 1942. The first view is without personnel, the other has at least 24 members of the armed forces in view. The vehicles, obviously the same in both views, are headed by three Harley Davidson motorcycles, which will form the escorting out-riders. In the left-hand column the front three-tonner and the subsequent nine trucks are Type 13 Cab Canadian Chevrolet C60L G/S. The middle column looks to be comprised of a few CMPs and Diamond Ts with Transit Numbers in the Pearson's-allocated CMD 50,001 series. Few other details can be obtained from what appears in this closely packed formation, although the front one looks to be a Model 969 wrecker. The right-hand column has at least two Chevrolet C60L G/S trucks, with more CMPs behind. It is led however by a 980 Diamond T tractor, which was a turntable/fifth wheel version! All these vehicles would have been Canadian order trucks being delivered by the Royal Canadian Ordnance Corps (RCOC). It will be noted that these vehicles have become operational by the fact that the Bridge Plate has been fitted. Indeed, CMP vehicles fitted with the Type 13 cab often had the bridge plate mounted on what would normally have been the off-side headlight position. The point behind such Bridging Plates was to ensure that military vehicles were not directed to cross bridges that were too weak to support their weight. All military and civilian bridges were rated by the Royal Engineers and their Canadian counterparts as to the maximum load they could support. these CMPs were Class 9, which included the majority of the British three-ton trucks.*

Bottom Left: *Looking up Overbury Street from Smithdown Lane and Faulkner Street in March 1943. Note the roofless bomb-damaged building, plus the marble arch leading to the 'Mersey Marble Works'; on the left is the entrance to the railway goods yard. Signs also point the way to the Air Raid Shelter, The British Restaurant and an Emergency Water Supply 140 yards to the left. Visible are two Ford F60B Bofors lorries, probably before being re-built to self-propelled units as they lack trailers and a Type No.13 cab CMP following the Ford. The Jeep with a trailer to the left is most likely a Ford GPW.*

WARRINGTON
20
CED
179

Left: *Once again we have a picture taken at the junction of Faulkner Street and Smithdown Lane, looking down the eastern side of Smithdown Lane with the Phoenix Safe Works on the right, complete with an air-raid lookout shelter on the roof. The first street on the left is Carlisle Street (which also led to the second assembly plant between St. Arnaud Street and Angela Street), whilst that on the right is Aigburth Street. This March 1943 view emphasises that the streets of Liverpool were packed with traffic, which was not surprising when you consider that over 1,000 convoys arrived at the Port of Liverpool during the war, bringing vital supplies of foods, raw materials, men, aircraft and the military vehicles. Taking the civilian vehicles first we see Morris 10 and 12 saloons, plus a lorry and trailer from the fleet of Peter Walker & Sons. Ltd., Liverpool and Warrington. The make of the lorry is not really identifiable, but it carries the fleet number 154 and was registered CED 179 in 1937. Peter Walker was a member of a Scottish brewing family that settled in Liverpool and had a brewery in the centre and another at Warrington; his brother founded the city's Walker Art Gallery. With regard to the military vehicles, the left-hand column is led by a Bedford MW, and whilst we have no evidence to suggest that Pearson's actually bodied any MWs, they were not known to have done any work on the QLs either; although from this view and those on pages 42 and 43 we now have photographic evidence that they actually did. The column also contains at least two Allis Chalmers M6 gun tractors. Note the Canadian Ford GPW Jeep and the Ford F30B Bofors in the right-hand column. A lorry is also seen emerging from the front entrance to Pearson's premises, meanwhile lorries are being worked on in the exposed shed to the right; note the use of the tarpaulin over one end of the 'shed' to provide some kind of protection from the weather. Just one chimney from the former safe factory remains standing, although pre-war views of the same premises clearly show that this was just one of seven such structures.*

Top Right: *In a picture dating from December 1944, we see a view of the engine assembly bay in the Smithdown Lane premises, and in a part of the Milner safe factory that escaped the bomb damage. It will be noted that a number of six-cylinder engines are being refurbished on the benches; we are unsure if these are military re-builds or part of the refurbishment programme for former WD trucks that commenced in late-1944. It will be observed that this was quite a comprehensive machine shop, and it also had an engine test bed facility, upon which the re-built engines could be 'run in' before being fitted.*

Bottom Right: *In addition to repairing old packing cases, Pearson's also made new ones in part of the old Safe Works. These crates were used in conjunction with CKD vehicles that Pearson's were then exporting from Liverpool docks, notably to UK forces in North Africa, the Middle East, India and the Far East. This is also a view from December 1944, and it is believed was taken for use in a brochure that the company intended to produce once the war was over.*

Top Left: *In one of the remaining (smoked-stained) parts of the Phoenix Safe Works, the photograph has recorded work-in progress on several 2½-ton Four Wheel Drive Auto Company FWD Model HAR-1 trucks. The HAR-1 trucks were supplied under Ministry of Supply Demand S/M 2330 (1,664) and 2721 (30), which were then used as G/S load carriers (some with smoke generator equipment). However, another quantity were acquired in 1943 under S/M 2930. Other HAR-1 chassis were equipped (as seen on these pages) with a Bros rotary snow plough for the dispersal of snow from aerodrome runways etc.*

Bottom Left: *Here we have a rear-three-quarter view of a Bros Sno-go snow blower on the Four Wheel Drive Auto Company FWD Model HAR-1 chassis, showing the self-contained Climax engine compartment with rear radiator in 1941. These were probably allocated Royal Air Force serial numbers rather than WD-style Census Numbers; indeed the RAF still had some in their inventory until the 1960s! The direction of disposal could be controlled to either side of the machine. Depending on the depth of snow, the operating speed was from ½ to 3mph but they could clear a path 78" wide. The petrol engine at the back was a Coventry Climax R6, which was mounted directly on to the rear chassis members. the engine itself was given minimum outer protection with removable access panels. However, this made for an odd-looking vehicle, especially when viewed from the rear, as the wheels, the near-side-mounted petrol tank and off-side-mounted spare wheel were all exposed. David Bracksome who drove these in the Ardenes Forest recalls that: - "They were murder when in convoy on account of the mud thrown up by the rear wheels of the vehicle line-ahead."*

Right: *This front-three-quarter view of the HAR-1 was also taken on the bombed-out site at the junction of Smithdown Lane and Queensland Street in January 1941. In the background we see what appears to be a Diamond T 969 heavy wrecker with Gar Wood crane. The picture is particularly useful as it clearly shows how the Sno-Go system worked. The power from the 'donkey' engine was transmitted to the rotary parts of the plough, namely rotor and rake; firstly by multiple V-belt drive from the engine to a layshaft and then through transmission shafts beneath the truck to an enclosed spiral drive on the rotor assembly; a chain-drive from the rotor assembly operated the rake. There was also a hydraulic system operating at 750lb/sq inch supplied from a gear-type pump driven by the Climax engine. The hydraulic system's functions were: a) raising or lowering the entire plough assembly; b) pivoting the rake through an arc to break up large drifts; or c) swinging the deflectors to discharge the snow to the right or left of the vehicle. The system was controlled by hand levers in the cab. The cab was however, a relatively basic affair offering only limited protection for the crew, and with just a canvas roof and door. Given that the work these vehicles were expected to carry out, namely snow clearance, the provision of an enclosed cab might have been more appropriate.*

CKC 548
GENERAL MOTORS

Left: *In the autumn of 1940, Pearson's registered at least four (possibly five) 1939-40 Model left-hand-drive GMC tractor units for their own use. These were possibly converted from what had been 'diverted orders', which General Motors Ltd had originally destined for France or Belgium. These orders were then sent to the Bamber Bridge facility near Preston, where they were assembled and allocated to 'Essential Users' by the Ministry of Supply. Pearson got an allocation of five, but the notes say that this was later amended to four, and we know that the registration sequence was at least CKG 545-8. Whatever the actual number of units allocated, Pearson's used these trucks to carry CKD crates from the docks to the storage sites or the works, and also used them to deliver trailers that they had assembled. A typical example of a semi-trailer supplied by Pearson's is this one by Bartlett, which was fitted with a Grain Elevator powered by a Caterpillar diesel engine. The Ministry of Food Production used these units to lift imported grain out of ships into silos.*

Above: *A right side view of the other trailer. Note the spare wheel under the trailer. These views date from 1943, when the grain elevators were being built.*

Right: *A rear view of a further trailer showing the 'BARTLETT' maker's plate and the 20mph plate. Although the background of these photographs has been obscured by order of the official censor, the location is Oliver Street.*

Top Left: *Here we have a series of three pictures that all date from November 1941, which show trucks being assembled in the corrugated asbestos sheet-clad building between Angela Street and St. Arnaud Street. The first view shows a line of 'Truck 15-cwt 4 x 4 Personnel' vehicles being assembled, which have been supplied by the White Motor Company of Cleveland, Ohio, under Demand S/M 2277. The leading truck has Census Number Z 5809309 from the batch Z 5809258 to 5809757. The other batches under the contract were Z 4953034 to 4955463; 5328601 to 5329000 and 5515784 to 5517049. On the right appear to be GMC CCKW-353 6 x 6 lorries with stake bodies. It will be seen that some of the CKD crates were unpacked inside the workshop, and with these we can find evidence of the chassis main frame, the engine, the axles and wheel assemblies being un-crated inside the plant. It will be noted that many of the assembly line workers are either old men or young boys, although one female employee is also present. It will be further noted that a large banner has been erected proclaiming "Keep 'em Rolling - The Troops Need These Trucks." Similar slogans were quite commonplace in British factories, as exhortations like this were often designed to play on the workers' loyalty to King and Country; others were designed to make the women workers believe that they were supporting their loved ones who were fighting with the armed forces.*

Bottom Left: *This would appear to be another pair of assembly lines in the same building, which was locally known as the Bridge Works (although no-one can recall why), in which that on the left-hand-side is seen working on the refurbishment of Longbridge-built Austin K2/Y ambulances towards the end of 1943. A large number of these were shipped back from North Africa, to be refurbished at Liverpool in readiness for further service after the Normandy Invasion. In the foreground, the right-hand line is occupied with vehicle components being removed from packing crates by small electric cranes.*

Right: *This further view again taken inside the 'Bridge Works' in October 1943, shows that numerous vehicles of various types are either under assembly or refurbishment (CCKW-353s right). Note the five-ton travelling gantry crane by Aabacas Engineering Ltd. of Birkenhead, which can be seen above the White Scout Car on the right. In the foreground are various wooden bodies being constructed to different military patterns, because the majority of the vehicles that were shipped to Liverpool were devoid of timber bodies as a weight-saving measure. Helen Street, who as a young widow worked at Pearson's, recalls that: "The wood used for the bodies also came from Canada, and at times in 1942 there was not enough material for us to body all the chassis that were arriving, later it was a case of too much timber and not enough chassis, due to problems with the Atlantic crossings." There appears to be a line of Austin 3-ton K3/YB G/S lorries on the building's left side being assembled and refurbished (see P.19) one of which has been fitted with a camouflaged canvas cover.*

AABACAS
ENGINEERING COMPANY LIMITED
BIRKENHEAD
5 TONS

KIT
OUT
RAF
7

Left: *Once again we have a representative selection of three images from another series of official photographs taken by the firm of Stuart Bale, this time in March 1944. The views here feature a WOT1 (RAF 109223) supplied by Ford of Dagenham as an 'Equipped Chassis', which are sometimes referred to as a Fordson. This version had a normal control chassis-cowl, but was then given a County Commercial Cars Limited six-wheel 'Sussex' conversion (the rear four wheels were driven) with 7 1/2" articulation and special Power Take-Off unit. It had 10.50 x 16 tyres and the engine was the standard Ford 30hp V8. The chassis was bodied separately and equipped with a basic 'roadster' style cab, to create a 'Monitor for airfield crash duties'. The MoS and Air Ministry placed similar orders for chassis with closed cabs, General Purpose Carriers, ambulances, barrage balloon winch lorries, and airfield crash tenders, though only the latter had the special PTO. The vehicle seen here is obviously not a new one, as can be determined from the scuffed paint work, small dents in the wing and the staining around the water tank. It is therefore believed that, like the Austin K2 ambulances, Pearson's had been contracted to rebuild ex-North African vehicles for further service in Europe in 1944.*

Top Right: *The version of the W0T1 seen here is the RAF's 1944 monitor conversion vehicle, which was a development and improvement of the original Ford crash tender; indeed, 50% of the 350 monitors that were built were conversions of the original series. They carried 300-gallons of water and 100-gallons of foam compound. The pump was a self-contained unit, which was not operated via a power take off but independently powered by a 30hp Ford V8 engine. The engine is seen situated between the monitor's 'crane' and water tank, and located in its own protective housing.*

Bottom Right: *A rear-three-quarter view of the monitor conversion, showing clearly the girder-like structure that many people refer to as a crane. This elevating platform was not designed for rescue purposes at all, for when in operation and fully elevated it resembled a trolley bus tower wagon. A fireman would then scuttle up the tower and stand on a platform from where he could conduct his operations. This gave a 90-degree perpendicular position to enable the firefighter to be positioned on a square platform at the head of the tower, from where he could direct a jet of foam onto a stricken aircraft. This was particularly essential with the RAF's larger four-engined aircraft such as the Lancaster, Halifax and Stirling bombers. In addition to the platform monitor, two other monitors were mounted on the base of the ladder platform. For that era it was a formidable weapon in the fireman's arsenal. For further details, see the Nostalgia Road book* Airport Crash Tenders ISBN 9781903016 18 3 *by Ron Henderson.*

Above: *This crate being opened in the yard behind the Falkner Street housing complex adds to the mystery of the CDSW '30cwt 6 x 4 Breakdown' L trucks handled by Pearson's. At first we wondered if the other images showed a truck or series of trucks that had been sent for refurbishment, like the Austin K2s and K3s seen on previous pages. However, when this partially-crated view turned up, it became obvious that Semi-Knocked-Down vehicles were handled on Merseyside. From the stencilling on the outside of this Morris-Commercial CDSW Breakdown truck, we can see it carries Census Number L 4551527, one of the same batch to Contract V.3957. Meanwhile, careful examination of the photographic register shows that this view dates from Monday 5th June 1941.*

Left and Right: *Here we have two of the official photographs taken by Stuart Bale in Liverpool, which are consecutively numbered and taken in April 1944 and therefore probably show the same vehicle. It is a model CDSW '30-cwt 6 x 4 Breakdown', produced by Morris Commercial Cars Ltd at Adderley Park, Birmingham. This one is L 4551516, one of the batch L 4551434 to 4551531, which had been supplied to Contract V.3957, which covered several MCC CDSW types. It is not known why they were being handled by Pearson's, but it has been suggested that these were part of an order that was initially crated for shipping and intended for the Far East, but were subsequently diverted for assembly at Liverpool after the Fall of Singapore in February 1941.*

MORRIS BREAKDOWN LORRY

This Page: *Three 1942 views of a gasoline-powered LT50 (or LT56) forklift from the Towmotor Forklifts Corporation of Cleveland, Ohio. These were acquired by the MoS to Demand S/M 2896, although the US Army used several Towmotor models. The capacity was in the 5-6,000lb class. Note the optional extension backrest and the stowed forks. The engines were probably Continental units with Delco six-volt generators. They have been described as being over-engineered, but they only had a drive-shaft brake, which required caution on wet ramps.*

Right: *These views show a Carloader 'Multitractor' High Telescopic Lift Fork Truck (possibly 4,000lb) by Clark Tructractor of Battle Creek, Michigan and supplied to S/M6325. The forks have been stowed and 'Lift OK' suggests that the truck has been tested and is awaiting delivery. The location of the photo shows that it is adjacent to the wall of Crown Street Goods Yard; the barbed wire has not been fitted yet on top of the recycled brick extension to the stone wall, and this dates the view to early-1942. By 1939, Clark had developed a new line of heavy duty lift trucks and towing tractors that were especially useful to the military. In the early-1940s, monthly production at the Trucktractor division shot as high as 2,500, up from the 1939 average of about 60. The war obviously paid huge dividends for by 1943, the company's sales were $77 million, up from $12.5 million four years earlier. The Carloader was intended for use on hard-surfaced areas and became the backbone of many companies' material handling systems.*

CLARK
CLARK

CLARK
CLARK

Top Left: *In the background of this picture showing the crating yard at the side of the Phoenix Safe Works, we see a batch of five Clark forklift trucks waiting to be delivered to Royal Air Force 22 Maintenance Unit in Carlisle, on a flat-bed truck from the firm of C. G. Stamper of Culgaith near Penrith; a firm who were loyal Atkinson customers for many years. We are unsure of the date this was taken (probably between (April 1942 and February 1944) but the mobile cranes seen alongside date from 1941-2, when 250 Karry Kranes were shipped over to work in English ports, where bomb damage had made unloading ships virtually impossible.*

Bottom Left & Below: *This pair of views illustrate a 13,000lb Ross Series 15 (possibly a Model SL), which was assembled at Liverpool in August 1942, and made to a design previously supplied to the US Navy by the Ross Carrier Company, Benton Harbor, Michigan. These were acquired for use by the British military forces by the MoS under Demand S/M 6180. They employed a 209 cubic inch, six-cylinder 75bhp engine, and were very powerful for their size. It has been discovered that a batch of 50 such machines were supplied to the Admiralty, for use by the Fleet Air Arm. Other examples were supplied with torpedo handling forks; some of which went to a supply base that was located in the New Forest, according to LTO David Wallings, who's mother ironically worked assembling these trucks at the Pearson plant in Smithdown Lane.*

Top and Bottom Right: *This Clarkat Aircraft Carrier Tug was also produced by the Clark Equipment Company of Buchanan, Michigan, and acquired by the MoS in 1942. The Clarkat 'B' tow tractor was manufactured from 1940 to '45 and had a drawbar pull rating of either 2,000lbs or 2,600lbs depending on the model. The wall in the background of the right-hand picture is on Faulkner Street, with the Crown Street railway yards beyond.*

Below: *This image shows Crown Street Yard of the Liverpool & Manchester Railway as it was in March 2007! When the railway opened throughout in 1831, locomotive-hauled trains only ran as far as Edge Hill. For the last leg of the journey, winding engines hauled the coaches by a cable up an incline passing through a short tunnel below Overbury Street. In the opposite direction, coaches ran by gravity down to Edge Hill. However, before the line opened, it was obvious that the western terminus would be inconvenient for the docks. To rectify this, a tunnel was opened from Crown Street to the Wapping Docks in 1830; entering a portal between Lissant and Sirdar streets, it ran down a steep 1:48 gradient. The tunnel was an impressive 2,216-yards (2,030 metres) long, through which wagons were cable-hauled up from the Wapping Docks and descended by gravity for 65-years until 1895/6 when it went over to locomotive haulage. The air shaft of the Wapping Tunnd is still extant, as seen in the picture below; this is taken from more or less the same vantage point, but in a similar direction to that shown on the title page of this book.*

Top and Bottom Left: *This is a 'Chance Light' airfield lighting unit mounted on a British-built Brockhouse trailer. The engine-driven generator is in the box housing, and there is a double 'Chance Light' fitted, one on top of the other. The protective sliding doors are shut across the two glass light covers, so making its use somewhat hidden. At the very top, the chimney like protrusion is in fact the housing for the red glass illuminated 'obstruction' light.*

Right: *An official photograph of a Kreiger 'Trailer five-ton four-wheel Smoke Generator' supplied under Demand S/M 6071. It is one of the batches X 5306747 to 5306776; 5443652 to 5443770; 5443821 to 5443951 and 5814851 to 5815050, which in turn were used with FWD HAR-1 trucks supplied under S/M 2330 and 2721. The generators were widely used with anti-aircraft units and also by the army to provide smoke screens. The location is once again in Smithdown Lane, right where the junction with Queensland Street was to be found. When compared to the period photographs seen in this book, much of this area is unrecognisable today.*

Below: *Looking from the former parapet of the railway bridge, complete with distinctive concrete panel, which was still extant in 2007, we look in the opposite direction to what remains of Smithdown Lane, at the end of which a relatively modern housing estate now occupies the former Milner's Phoenix Safe Works site.*

SMOKE GENERATOR. S/M 6071.

X 5578887
S/M 6216

X5578887
S/M 6216

S/M6216
X5578887

Opposite Page, Top & Bottom Left and Top Right: *This trailer carried Census Number X 5578887 and was acquired under Demand S/M 6216. It is another 'Trailer eight-ton four-wheel' from the batch X 5578790 to 5578907, but built by Cahn in the USA. Compare the drawbar, ramps and side-chains on that model with those on the Fruehauf version on this page; note that the vehicle seems to have highway-tread tyres all round.*

Opposite Page Bottom Right: *This appears to be a 'Trailer two-wheel Dolly Converter' supplied by Truck Engineering Company to Demand SM/CA2420 in the batches X 6246802 to 6247001 and 6269421 to 6269620. The design originally came from the American Navy, who wanted the facility to enable fifth-wheel trailers to be towed by hook-equipped drawbar vehicles.*

This Page: *Whilst this trailer looks very similar to those opposite, you can clearly see that it is carrying Census Number X 5873009, to Demand S/M 6194, and this indicates that it was manufactured by the Fruehauf Trailer Company in the USA. They were officially 'Trailer Eight-ton four-wheel' and allocated Census Numbers X 5872965 to 5873014. Note the drawbar arrangement and the ramps. The tyres in this instance are military cross-country tread. Going from the pattern of the cobbles and the pavement flags, all these views are taken in either Crown Street or Oliver Street.*

S/M.
2574.
X 5843553

Left and Above: *This trailer, X 5843553, carries chalk marks that show it to be for the Demand 'S/M 2574', however the Census List actually quotes S/M 2754, so we must assume the hand-lettering to be incorrect. It is one of ten Hobbs 'Trailer four/six-ton four-wheel', from the batch X 5843527 to 5844136 that were assembled for British use by Pearson's: note the highway tyres. Following World War II, 150 of these trailers were allocated by the US Government for the primary strategic 'Sealift' mission, which was designed to rapidly move men and equipment to Europe to defend the 'West' in case of an attack by the Soviet Warsaw Pact forces. The central front was 3,600 miles away and 'Sealift' would be provided by over 600 NATO merchant vessels and an active US Navy merchant fleet that still numbered 578 major ships. The Hobbs trailers were sent to ports such as Rotterdam and Bremen on account of the amount of goods they could carry.*

Right: *Here we see two further views of the 'Ben Hur' Trailers that were built by Willys-Overland Motors Inc of Toldeo, Ohio. The one featured here, X 5819132 (see also page 15), is a 'Trailer one-ton two-wheeled G/S' to Demand S/M 6288 fitted with cross-country tyres. These trailers were used with the F60B Bofors CMP trucks as well as Jeeps. The batches were: X 581901 to 5819290; 5837066 to 5837165; 5837216 to 5837425; 6109440 to 6109639; 6168654 to 6168853 'and/or Generator' and 6259138 to 6259469. When the F60B Bofors were converted to self-propelled units in 1944, the trailers would have presumably been surplus and either re-allocated or repaired for further use! Once again the location for the pictures is on Smithdown Lane, with the 'throat' of the Crown Street Goods Yard located on the opposite side of the wall.*

Another 1943 view from the junction of Overbury Street (on the left), with the eastern end of Smithdown Lane running up to the right. Visible are both open and original closed-cab Diamond T 981 tractors. They have probably been supplied to S/M 2147, and the front one on the right side of the road is pulling a 'Rogers type' 40-ton trailer. On the left is an Allis-Chalmers M6. The lady is driving a Canadian-order Ford GPW Jeep (left), as evidenced by the 'CMD' prefix, which stood for 'Canadian Mechanization Depot'. This was also an assembly sequential number used by assembly plants before WD-style Census Numbers were applied in the Canadian series; by contrast the Jeep on the right is a British order Ford GPW (M5844964 (S/M 2946). There is also a Ford F.15A CMP with square roof hatch (Z 5836223) a Ford F60S 'Tractor 4 x 4 Light AA (H6100380) and a White Scout Car. Note the view through the 'Marble Arch' that leads into what were the Mersey Marble Works. A sign, which has been censored in this picture, would have read 'John Stubbs & Sons - Marble Experts and Craftsmen. This firm, formerly of Crown Street, supplied various types of stone for a wide variety of applications, including many civic buildings and the portals of the Mersey Tunnel.

M5844964

Above: *This is a February 2007 view of the Mersey Marble Work site that is seen on the previous two pages. These works used to make the thick white marble butchers and display slabs, such as those found in Galkoff's Kosher Butchers in Pembroke Place. They also made the granite column that formed part of the war memorial in front of the Cunard Building at the Pier Head, along with many of the marble fittings in some of the great ships and trans-Atlantic liners of the White Star Cunard Line. They also provided much of the finishing touches for the Mersey Road Tunnel.*

Left: *This 1941 picture is taken in the 165, Smithdown Lane premises before it was bombed in May that year. The view is captioned as 'GMC rear bodies 1941', and would appear to show wooden G/S bodies being constructed for GMC chassis. Possibly these were either ex-French contract lorries, or CCKW-353 chassis.*

Right: *This view inside part of the fire-damaged Phoenix Safe Works demonstrates the variety of vehicles handled in 1945! On the left is an International Harvester M14 'Truck 15-cwt Half Tracked Personnel' with the rear of another on the right. There is also Number 13 Cab CMPs: a three-tonner long wheelbase, probably C60L, and a 15-cwt model. The Ford GPW has civilian trade plates. The twin-rear wheeled Fordson tractor is towing a wooden G/S body with benches; a chalked 'headboard' proclaims double liberty referring to the campaigns in both Europe and the Far East.*

CAUTION
LEFT HAND
DRIVE
520
GXB 382
L46 76701
Z530606
Z 5517514
055 LV

CABLE
VOLTS

Left: *We initially thought that this was yet another post-war view of vehicle refurbishment in the old Safe Works. However, subsequent information from people who were then in the employ of Pearson's, confirms this to have been taken in what was left of the bomb-damaged premises at 165, Smithdown Lane. It shows several GMC $2^{1}/_{2}$-ton CCKW-353 6 x 6 lorries being refurbished. A Model 1609 cab (with an aperture in roof) has already been removed for attention, whilst the chassis frame to its left seems to have been, or has become, distorted. Four of those ex-employees recall that a total of 56 examples of this kind of truck were sent back to Liverpool for re-building. The majority were all badly damaged, and several had to be cannibalised for spares, but this was a time when every vehicle was needed to be got ready in time for use in the spring of 1944 ahead of the 'Second Front'. This view is also interesting, because it shows work being carried out on the first floor, and the ground floor below can be seen over cast-iron railings to the right. Meanwhile, the windows on the left show distinct signs of smoke-staining as a result of air raid damage.*

Top Right & Overleaf: *A stunning 1945 view from the junction of Smithdown Lane and Overbury Street going to the left and Falkner Street going to the right. From left to right we see two International Harvester M14s 'Truck 15-cwt, a half Tracked Personnel'. The GPW 'Jeep' is a Ford 'Car 5-cwt 4 x 4', and the front one is being driven by Doreen Parr (nee Traverse), one of the Subscribers to this book. Also from Ford are the three-ton 123" wheelbase 4 x 4 CMP Model C39QB F60B Bofors; these have been re-built or converted from the self-propelled tractors (S.P.M. 40mm). The armoured cars M 4709x35 and 4709359 are British Humber 'Car 4 x 4 Light Recce MkIII' to MoS Contract VM.4855. The Allis-Chalmers M6 H 6164828 is to Demand S/M 6458 and the Diamond T 981 H5587679 to Demand S/M 2147. There is also a Diamond T 969 four-ton wrecker ['Tractor, Breakdown, Medium'] under the roof in the yard, whilst next to it are three Mack Model LMSW-57 Heavy Wrecker or 'Tractor 6 x 4 Break Down' to Demand S/M 2109. In the yard are two of the 1940-41 GMC Tractor-Trailer units, with the Caterpillar diesel-powered grain elevator sets on flat semi-trailers. In the extreme background in the yard appears to be a Forward Control or COE GMC, and a FWD HAR-1 4 x 4 with a front-mounted snow blower nearby. To the right of the FWD is a mighty Mack FCSW 'Truck, 30-ton 6 x 4 Dump'; acquired in 1943 for the Ministry of Works under Lend-Lease for coal excavation etc. Finally, there are various Ford and Chevrolet CMPs, with both square and round roof hatches, including Z 5452424, a Canadian Chevrolet Model 8421 C15 'Truck 15-cwt. 4 x 2 G/S' to Demand S/M 6050 and a Ford F60L or Chevrolet C60L G/S truck.*

Bottom Right: *This is the site of the above picture in 2007, with the houses shown here occupying the old crating yard. the view is taken from the junction of Overbury Street and Smithdown Lane, with the road on the right being Faulkner Street, down which the 1945 vehicles seen above are heading towards.*

EARSONS · L·POOL
Z6111184
Z6111136
S5582

Z6111128
M5845024
M5845584
Z5452424

Having been shipped from Newport News, Virginia, these Partially Knocked Down (PKD) Diamond T trucks are being un-crated from 'Gamma' 'Twin Unit Packs' (TUPs) in 1944, having been brought up from Liverpool Docks to the Crown Street Goods Yard. Two trucks were packed into a series of crates. One crate held the chassis with the axles, engine, radiator, scuttle, mudguards, and winch in place. Eight tyres and wheels were mounted on top of the chassis; three were placed on the crate floor under the running board. Two cabs were supplied in a separate single crate. The ballast truck bodies were also supplied separately (two to a crate) direct from the body builders. The drawbar trailers were supplied as 'Single-Unit Packs' (SUPs) although the trailer was in fact packed in three crates. One carried the frame and drawbar, one contained the front-wheel assembly and miscellaneous items, the third contained the rear axle and trunnion assemblies. It is assumed that the semi-trailers were also shipped in two crates. This the photograph is taken in the 'Un-crating yard' between the old Phoenix Safe Works and Windsor Gardens, with the 1941 extension seen in the background. We also see one of the firm's Hyster $3^{1}/_{2}$-ton four-wheel mobile cranes that were supplied to the MoS under Contract S/RE/29 (Census Numbers 4614958 to 4614999). It is lifting the first crate with the chassis etc, whilst to the left is a crate containing a Chrysler of Canada Dodge D60S Tipper T-110-L-6, supplied under S/M 6068.

W.D.M.T.
SPLY/MECH 6068
CASE
GROSS
TARE
LENGTH
HEIGHT
DIAMOND T MOTOR CAR CO
558
GROSS 2000
TARE
LENGTH
WIDTH
HEIGHT

A1210147

Left: *Pearson's occupied a number of cleared bomb sites, one of which was adjacent to the premises of W. E. Wilson & Faquharson Commercial Motor Engineers, Liverpool 7, who were sub-contractors to Pearson's. These stabling sites were used for two distinct types of vehicle; namely those that had been erected from CKD crates, and were awaiting despatch to their receiving base, and older WD vehicles that were shipped back to Liverpool for refurbishment. Two distinct periods are associated with the refurbishment work; the spring of 1940 (after the fall of Dunkirk) and the Summer of 1943 (after German and Italian troops surrendered in North Africa on 13th May that year). This view dates from late-1943 and shows around 30 Austin K2/Y 'Ambulance 4 x 2' (four-stretcher) vehicles awaiting refurbishment work, some of which is obviously being done in this view; note the lady posing by the lead ambulance with a paintbrush in her hand, whilst engineers have obviously been at work tuning the engines. Also of interest are the variations in the Red Cross markings, with at least two having large crosses on the sides and cabs. The ambulance seen here would be to contracts A 2271 and A 2939, and would have had Census Numbers A1209218 to A 1212286.*

Top Right: *As stated, Pearson's were allowed to purchase and refurbish ex-WD vehicles from late-1944 onwards, and here we have two pictures of some of the earlier examples. These are early rebuilds of the Number 12 Cab 15-cwt Chevrolet C15 4 x 2 trucks, which have been converted to two different van designs. The pair are seen outside the Shaw Street Garage, but it is interesting to compare its May 1945 appearance with the pre-war photographs seen earlier in this book. In the case of the left truck it has a new coach-built cab and doors, whereas the one on the right retains its original cab. Note the road tyres, mirror on the right truck and different headlights. Whilst it is not possible to ascertain which Demand these were originally acquired under, late production under the large order S/M 2002 included No. 12 Cab chassis, as did all those supplied under S/M 2031 for 'G/S Trucks' in addition to Canadian orders for assembly in the UK. The left-hand truck seen here can also be found on page 84, where it is shown in its fully painted guise for a delivery van in service of Singleton & Cole, 17, Hanover Street, Liverpool 1; manufacturers of mentholated snuff.*

Bottom Right: *This 1946 view, taken in Oliver Street, shows a 1941-2 Model 8421 15-cwt 4 x 2 Chevrolet C15 (similar to that seen above) re-built by Pearson's. This view confirms that it has a coach-built ice cream van body, incorporating a new cab and doors and ash frame under aluminium panels. This vehicle was seen for many years on the sea front around New Brighton on the opposite side of the Mersey. Note the ventilation holes either side of the radiator, which opened 'Alligator-style', and smaller wheels than the 30-cwt and 3-tonners [9.00 x 13]. This truck has a Ford CMP square mesh grille and keeps its front brush guard, although its retention on an ice cream van is puzzling.*

Left: & Right: *This was a Number 12 Cab Chevrolet C8 Model 8420 'Truck eight-cwt 4 x 2' supplied under Demand S/M 2029, and then re-built by Pearson's as a Liverpool Salvage Corps tender with a completely new body. The registration was issued in Liverpool in the Spring of 1946. This view from the back of the vehicle, gives a fascinating interior shot of the body showing storage racks and bench seat with rear padding for personnel. It also shows the rear step and running plate. A fully detailed account of the Salvage Corps can be found in the Nostalgia Road book* Fire Engines of North West England, *by Robert F Bonner ISBN 9781903016 38 1. The Salvage Corps was an organisation sponsored by insurance companies to provide a support resource to the Liverpool Fire Brigade. Briefly stated this organisation did a great deal of work alongside the municipal fire brigades in order to prevent additional fire or water damage following an incident, thus reducing the damage and insured losses.*

From many of the pictures in this book, it is quite obvious that Liverpool was a major target for the German Luftwaffe. The direct attacks on the dock can be readily understood, given their being the main receiving point for the Atlantic convoys, but some readers may find it hard to understand why the Edge Hill area was so heavily blitzed. The answer lies in the annals of railway history, for as we have already discussed on page 61, Crown Street was the western terminus of the Liverpool & Manchester Railway, the world's inter-city line.

The cable-haulage arrangements mentioned earlier continued until on 15th August 1836, when the line was extended down to Lime Street Station by means of a second tunnel from Edge Hill, and this was supplemented by a further tunnel a few years later, as substantial re-modelling of the layout around Edge Hill took place in the 1840s. The two Lime Street tunnels entered a portal just to the east of Smithdown Lane, about 100-yards north of the Corporation Stables. At first these tunnels were cable-hauled, but if they went over to locomotive haulage, they would need to be ventilated. So, in March 1869, the LNWR's Chief Mechanical Engineer, John Ramsbottom, patented a system for mechanical ventilation. This was installed in the tunnels during 1870-1 to allow the replacement of endless-rope haulage by locomotive power by venting the smoke from within the bores. The resulting lines were thereafter a potential choke-point, that, if successfully bombed, could have blocked off the city's main rail links.

Goods traffic continued to be handled at Crown Street for the next 30-years, especially coal and agricultural traffic. Though Hitler failed to close the goods yard, British Rail managed to that for themselves in May 1972, when the facility was withdrawn. The site was duly landscaped in 1980 and today, only a few railway traces remain.

SALVAGE
CORPS
GLV 16

RS 375

Left: *A post-war re-build of a 15-cwt 4 x 2 Chevrolet C15, with the later Number 13 Cab, was converted by Pearson's to form a Luton Van and re-built for the Bootle Co-operative Society Furnishing Department in February 1946. Note the sliding driver's door windows and the new integrated cab with a revised, almost vertical, windscreen arrangement and a single driver's side windscreen wiper. The front radiator guard and bumper have been re-painted gloss black. as has the chassis, but the wheels appear to have been sprayed in grey (with the tyres left on), like the rest of the van. However, once again the military brush guard and the heavy duty 'D' shackles have been retained. The vehicle had previously been a Royal Signals allocation, and presumably fitted with a 'house-type' body on the back. The photograph's location is unclear but it may have been taken on the site of Pearson's former 165, Smithdown Lane premises, where the remaining buildings were finally demolished in early-1945. If this supposition is correct, we think that the road on the right is Cardwell Street; yet, despite electronically enlarging the picture, the street sign on the top right building has proved unreadable. The only other consideration is that this may alternatively be the site outside the factory of W. E. Wilson & Faquharson Commercial Motor Engineers. The location of that firm's premises has also remained a mystery, despite a search of pre-war trade directories, but they are thought to have been located off Overbury Street, possibly around Hume Street and Ewart Street.*

Top & Bottom Right: *Another 8-cwt 4 x 2 Chevrolet C8 Model 8420 CMP with Number 12 Cab, re-built with a new bumper and a completely new wooden frame Station Wagon style body with new doors. Note the gloss black painted road tyres replacing the military style, the lack of a radiator brush guard and the internal seating. This conversion was made for the Earl of Strathmore as an 'Estate Car'. As a Utility, which other 'woody' vehicles were then classified, it would be subject to the commercial speed limit on public roads. In the 18th century, the 9th Earl of Strathmore married a wealthy heiress, Mary Eleanor Bowes and subsequently became Lord Bowes after inheriting estates in England. He then adopted the name of Bowes-Lyon as the family name, and into his family line was born Elizabeth Angela Marguerite Bowes Lyon on 4th August 1900; the ninth of ten brothers and sisters. Those who know British history will appreciate that in 1920 this great lady married Prince George, son of King George V, and as a result became the Queen of Britain and the British Empire, following the abdication of her brother-in-law Edward VII and the subsequent Coronation of her husband as George VI on 12th May, 1937. The order for this shooting truck to be used on the grouse moors around Barnard Castle was quite a prestigious job for Pearson's, so it is little wonder that the 'shooting brake' was featured in their post-war advertising; it is thought that the vehicle finished its working days on the Glamis Castle estate in Scotland. The pictures were both taken outside the original park gate of Sefton Park, which was to be found on Aigburth Drive at the point where it lead up to the crossroads with Ullet Road.*

CHEVROLET
PRODUCT OF
GENERAL MOTORS
LTD.
Ex W·D· Rebuilds
by
Pearsons of Liverpool
Constructional Engineers
McIntyre & Sons Ltd
Stanhope Street, Liverpool
W. EVANS, FLINT.
WHOLESALE TOBACCONIST
W. EVANS
Bank Buildings
Church St
Tele FLINT 2200
James Addey & Co
51, Old Hall St
Liverpool 3.
THORNTON
THORNTON LIVERPOOL
Take SINGLETON'S
Super Menthol SNUFF
& Breathe Freely
Singleton & Cole Ltd
17 Hanover Street
Liverpool 1
VIRGINIA
STEAM
LAUNDRY Ld.
Field Road.
NEW BRIGHTON
Telephones.
508 & 509 WALLASEY.
ESTABLISHED 1900.

Left: *An interesting advertisement from around 1947 showing that Pearson's had been appointed by General Motors Limited, to be official dealers for the former Ministry of Supply vehicles (and also Canadian ones) that were acquired by GM Ltd under the 'SMMT Scheme'. The No.12 Cab Chevrolet Canadian Military Pattern trucks have all been re-bodied as vans by Pearson's or (top left) had a new tipper body added. The centre wooden station wagon is that referred to on the previous page. The other two (middle left and right) are a 1941-2 Model Chevrolet and a 1940 ex-French order GMC ACX-504 rebuilt as a flat-bed and dropside/tipper lorry respectively.This advert was not only reproduced in the major motoring magazines of the day, but it was also made into a postcard, of which hundreds were posted to the company's potential customer base as a method of advertising.*

This Page: *Here we see three March 1948 views of a refurbished three-ton GMC ACKWX-353 162" wheelbase 6 x 6 lorry, which was the forerunner of the famous CCKWX-353/CCKW-353 or 'Jimmy'. It was just one of around 1,000 3-ton G/S lorries acquired under Demand S/M 2009. These were mainly diverted French orders that were supplied for use in the UK, the Census Numbers applied were L 4457706 to 4458705. This one retains its original military radiator guard and has road tyres all round. It is believed that these vehicles are seen on the 165, Smithdown Lane site after it was cleared. The background has been 'painted out' or 'bleached' in these photographs, not for wartime secrecy, but so they could be used in adverts. The firm's original assembly site was just one of the many bomb sites in Liverpool, a city that suffered more from bombing during World War II than any other provincial British city, because of its strategic value to the nation in importing food and other supplies. There were around 15,000 blitzed sites in Liverpool!*

Left: *This series of four January 1946 photographs, taken outside the former Wilson & Farquarson works, show a GMC Model ACK-353 'Lorry 30-cwt 4 x 4 GS'. This was a French contract diverted to Britain (acquired under Demand S/M 2008), and as such was one of 1,500 lorries that were allocated in the UK Census Numbers. Some of these were rebuilt at GM Bamber Bridge in 1941. The cab on this one appears to be identical to that of the six-wheeler version.*

Top & Bottom Right: *Here we have two views of a post-war re-build, featuring a vehicle that is yet again an ex-French GMC order, but this time a Model ACX-504, 'Lorry three-ton 4 x 2'. It was one of 1,850 diverted and then acquired under Demand S/M 2010 and allocated Census Numbers L 445328 to 4455107. It has been converted to three-plank tipper, using EDBRO tipper gear.*

Below: *The same type of cab and chassis, this time with a much deeper four-plank tipper body and EDBRO gear. EDBRO was a Bolton-based firm, which took its name from the three founders, the Edward Brothers. The company's tipping gear products came rapidly to prominence during World War II, and much of the success can be attributed to Eric Tonge. At the outbreak of the war, there was a dramatic decline in private car use, and Tongue was invited to sell his garage business and join EDBRO as their Works Manager. By the end of the war, his management skills had taken the company far ahead of the rival tipping gear manufacturers in Britain and one of the leaders in its field world-wide.*

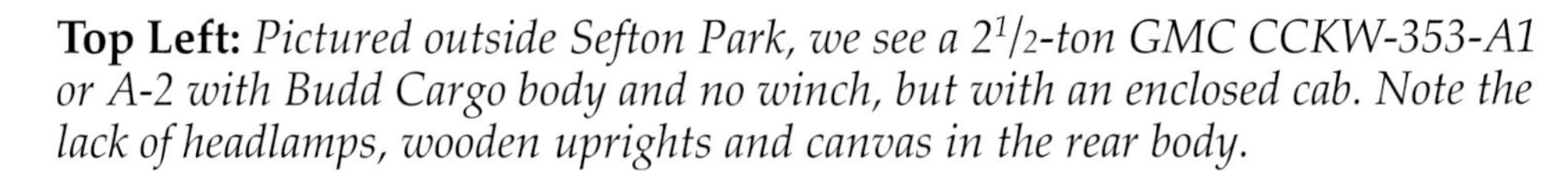

Top Left: *Pictured outside Sefton Park, we see a $2^{1}/_{2}$-ton GMC CCKW-353-A1 or A-2 with Budd Cargo body and no winch, but with an enclosed cab. Note the lack of headlamps, wooden uprights and canvas in the rear body.*

Bottom Left: *Again photographed outside the same park in December 1947, we find a CCKW-353-A1 or A-2, which is also fitted with a Budd Cargo body. However, this example is fitted with the weight-saving open cab, and would therefore have little appeal for civilian users in the post-war period. Pearson's got around this problem by stripping the backs off these lorries and treating them as chassis-cowl models and then fitted integral van bodies to them.*

Right: *This GMC was either a CCKW-353-A1 (if the chassis had split-type axles) or an A2 (if it had banjo-type axles), which has been fitted with a Budd Cargo body and closed cab, and is seen in almost 'as withdrawn' condition.*

Below: *A US-sourced 1942 Model military cab Chevrolet, 'One and a half-ton 4 x 4 Dump' Model NL 7116, which was refurbished by Pearson's with a glossy black chassis and wheels. The same basic body was shared with the Cargo versions, although this is missing bows and wooden uprights, and of course the canvas cover. Known examples were rated at two-ton or three-ton when registered.*

Left: *During the period 1945-7, Pearson's are known to have purchased over 2,500 ex-military vehicles, with supplies coming from British, Canadian and American disposal sales. However, not all the vehicles obtained came from the disposal sales, as Pearson's held a supply of around 400 un-crated vehicles along with about 200 other vehicles that had been sent back to Liverpool for refurbishment. In total, this made for well over 3,000 post-war 're-builds', with about ten per day being turned out between June 1945 and August 1946, the output had dropped to about ten per week during 1947 as new commercials vehicle chassis became more widely available to the vehicle body-builders. Here we see a January 1946 refurbishment of a Number 13 cab Model 8442. This was a Chevrolet C60s BRKD-3, -4 or -5 depending on whether the cab was articised, non-articised or winterised. It is a 'Lorry three-ton 4 x 4 derrick articised' or 'lorry three-ton 4 x 4 b/down'. The tubular structure was to enable a tarpaulin to be put over to make the truck look like a 'common or garden' G/S, which was a common tactic to 'camouflage' the specialist role it undertook. There were different types of configuration for these CMP wreckers, of which this seems to be the third type; it also has a Gar Wood CA5P crane. The body type is a bit difficult to determine but is believed to be a 4G2 and not a 4D1. The difference is that the 4D1 used POW [Petrol Oil Water] cans, which were used on both Holmes and Gar Wood examples. The 4G2 used English-made 'Jerry cans', and it was only used together with Gar Wood (4G1 bodies are the same as 4G2 with Jerry cans, but they only used together with Holmes cranes). The BRKD-3 was articised (to withstand temperatures of -40^{0}F while the BRKD-5 was winterised (-20^{0}F). The BRKD-3 also had the diluter system and the engine primer system, with the small tank underneath the drivers door. Note, in the photograph shown here, that tank is missing. However it has the diluter tank in the window frame, and also a cab heater, showing the de-froster in the window. In contrast the model BRKD-4 was not winterised or articised.*

Top Right: *Another January 1946 photograph shows a re-build, this time a GM of Canada Model 8443 Chevrolet C60L, which is fitted with a Number 13 cab and a Lindsay-type House body. Although this might appear to be an Ambulance body at first glance, it is in fact a former Royal Canadian Army Medical Corps three-ton Dental Van. As such the body is substantially different to the Chevrolet C60L and Ford F60L Ambulances that the British acquired. It will be seen that the headlamps have not yet been replaced.*

Bottom Right: *This would appear to be a partially-refurbished and repainted 'Lorry 3-ton 4 x 4 G/S' Chevrolet C60L, which if "Articised' was one of the batch Census Numbers L 5429530 to 5432050 to Demand S/M 6110 shown. Note the glossy black wheels and lack of canvas on the rear body hoops. Once again the headlamps have not yet been replaced, as they would need to be to make them 'road legal' as 'newly registered' vehicles in 1946.*

Top Left: *The Census Number H 5571028 confirms that this is a Number 13 Cab Chevrolet Model 8440 'Tractor 4 x 4 FA'FAT4 ddivered under Demand S/M 6064 in the batch H 5570919 to 5571047. Although this model design dates from late-1942 or early-1943, they were not actually assembled until late-1943 or 1944. Registration evidence has shown that re-built former Artillery Tractors were fitted out with cranes as recovery vehicles, or, using the hook/winch arrangement, as agricultural tractors! This picture was taken outside Sefton Park 1946; note the letter 'S' for radio suppression.*

Bottom Left: *A June 1946 photograph of a Chevrolet Model 8440 Gun Tractor FAT2 'Tractor 4 x 4 FA' with Number 12 Cab, 7B2 body awaiting re-build. The R/S' means 'Repair or Salvage', and '191' presumably means the 190th vehicle. Note the spare wheel location. It is queried whether this was one of the batch delivered under Demand S/M 2028 with bodies by (for instance) Gotfredson Limited of Windsor, Ontario? We have no evidence to suggest that Pearson's operated a canibalisation programme, such as that operated by General Motors at Southampton, where parts were robbed from one vehicle to repair compatible ones. At GM this was known as 'Ten In - Nine Out', whereby one vehicle was sacrificed to repair the other nine. As* Old Bill *stands forlornly in the Crown Street railway yard, it seems to indicate that a similar practice may have happened at Smithdown Lane. The wall behind FAT is the opposite side of the wall that we have seen on the left-hand side of the picture on the title page and several other views in the book.*

Right: *Here we have a Chevrolet C8A Model 8445 Heavy Utility Computer 8-cwt 4 x 4 Canadian Military Code H. U.-441-M, which was fitted out as a gunnery computer. We cannot say where this was assembled, but Pearson's did build a number of these vehicles that were supplied from the General Motors of Canada, Oshawa plant. Unusually, the bodies were made complete at Oshawa, and presumably these were sent in separate crates to the chassis and the cab. Interestingly, the Number 13 Cab is fitted with the round roof hatch and has a canvas cover. Up to Serial Number 2844513800, the reverse-angle windscreens opened just 30 degrees, but from thereon they opened 90 degrees. The screens in the body shielded the 'on the plot' tables. The spare wheel/tyre was located on the right side of the body. The wheels have hubs which enable the truck to be lifted with slings. There is no Census Number or other markings in this March 1946 picture, from which it will be observed that the vehicle has now received a new near-side headlamp and side lights. We have no idea as to whether or not this picture represents the final extent of Pearson's conversion work, or what further work might still need to be undertaken. It is difficult to understand why, if further work was to be done, the company would commission their commercial photographers, Stuart Bale, to take this picture. If any reader can tell us why, we would be extremely interested to hear from them!*

AES
TAKORADI
HARBOUR
Nº 1
AES TAKORADI
HARBOUR Nº 2

Both Pages: *These are part of a set of very unusual CMP photographs (taken in March 1947), showing a unit that looks very similar to CMP vehicles that were used as timber carriers in Australia and as Pipe Carriers elsewhere. They appear to show a Number 13 Cab C15A Model 8444 15-cwt 4 x 4 converted to a tractor unit with a rear, two-wheel trailer using three-ton truck wheels! The stencilling showing either AFS Takoradi Harbour No.1 on the tractor and No.2 on the trailer stands for the American Field Service on the Gold Coast in what is now Ghana. The town was on the route of the American supply flights to North Africa, via South America. These trucks could have been used for moving tree trunks, as Ghana was a major source of timber, but we know that similar designs of vehicles were used in Britain during the construction of the 'Operation Pluto' oil pipeline that ran from Liverpool to the Isle of Wight and was then taken across the Channel into France to support the Allied Invasion; the last section of pipe being laid under the English Channel in just ten hours. We know that Takoradi, complete with its deep water port, was important for its production of both hardwood and plywood, with a lot of the latter being used in aircraft production for the Royal Air Force. Note the three-ton rear axle with differential, and what appears to be a folding stay to steady the rear. Quite why these vehicles would have been sent back to Liverpool for refurbishment after the war is not clear, but the fact that they are being refurbished is testified to by the new headlight that has been fitted on Takoradi No.1.*

Top Left: *The level of refurbishment by Pearson's varied considerably, presumably to customer specification, as we can see from this Number 13 Cab 15-cwt 4 x 2 Chevrolet C15. It is seen here 're-built' as a Chassis-Cab ready for bodying. Allun Armstrong, who worked at Pearson's between 1944 and 1948 stated that he recalls: - "This vehicle was originally fitted with an integral body and cab and that this therefore needed replacing with a surplus cab from a condemned chassis. In this form it was supplied to Liverpool Corporation and was used at one of the City's water treatment works." Note the air cleaner above the front near-side wheel arch, the over-spray of black wheel paint on the tyres, black chassis paint and square roof hatch on the Number 13 Cab. The picture is taken in Sefton Park.*

Bottom Left & Right: *This civilian conversion of a 15-cwt 4 x 4 Number 13 Cab Chevrolet C15A has a hatch, and wooden G/S-style body with a canvas top. It can be seen that the military headlamp holes have been blanked over and instead there is now just one headlamp mounted on the left side! The truck does however retain its Chevrolet bow-tie grille badge and towing rings as well the radiator brush guard with its dual leaf supports. Note the front Chevrolet 'banjo' front axle design on these October 1950 views, both of which were taken in Sefton Park, and of course are very late in the period of post-war military vehicle restoration. Agnes Stubbs, who lived in the tenements in Falkner Street recalls getting 'odd jobs' with the company, which she did with other local girls after school and on Saturdays, for which they were paid six-pence per week (2.5p). In the war years, their tasks included 'waxing' the lorries that had been assembled in the Safe Works and then taken into the compound on Smithdown Lane. This task involved applying a paraffin-based wax oil, similar to that used in candle-making, and rubbing this into all the painted surfaces on the tin-work on the body and cab. Agnes stated that: - "The paint that was used on these trucks was very poor quality stuff - it often came off on your hands when you worked on the vehicles. I think they must have used any type of paint they could lay their hands on. We would put the wax on to the trucks with shoe-cleaning brushes and really had to rub it in hard. We often worked in the complete darkness, and we had no lights to help us, and sometimes we went on to about nine o-clock at night. Sixpence might not sound much today, but it was good money in those days, nobody ever worked Friday nights, but we all went to the Pay Office after school to get our money, then we went off to the pictures, had fish and chips afterwards and then went dancing. It was an exciting time to be a 14-year-old girl in Liverpool, but we always had to be in by half-past ten at night, and we were never allowed to walk home on our own. The streets had far more dangers in those days towards the end of the war than they had presented back in the days of the May Blitz. After the war, even though I had started work in the sweet factory, I still went and worked for Pearson's on a Saturday, when we had the job of cleaning the mud from the under-side of the ex-army lorries."*

Left: *The partially obliterated Census Number on this 1946 picture appears to be Z 5193674, but no such number was issued. This looks to be a Number 13 Cab Chevrolet C15 or C15A, so Z 5194641 to 5195730 would appear to be the nearest Census Numbers that fit. These numbers were for Chevrolet C15 'Truck 15-cwt 4 x 2 AA (20 mm)' to Demand S/M 2485 of 1942. Such Chevrolet CMPs, together with Ford F15s, were delivered to the same contract, and were originally fitted with VAN-6 bodies. Around 2,000 of these were converted by Dennis Motors Ltd. of Guildford to 20mm AA gun platforms and were fitted with gun-carriage-cum-mounts by Vauxhall Motors. It has clearly had the body removed, and different wheels added. Note the square roof hatch and single right-hand blackout headlight.*

Top & Bottom Right: *Two views of a 134" wheelbase No. 13 Cab three-ton 4x4 Chevrolet C60S chassis-cab, with what appears to be a single left-hand headlamp. The 158" w.b. C60L and F60L had a two-piece drive-shaft with an intermediate bearing rather than (as here) a direct connection to the transfer case.*

Below: *A frontal view of a 15-cwt Chevrolet post-war (fifth-wheel tractor) refurbishment wearing civilian headlamps and side lamps, after the near-side headlamp has been blanked out with a new disc screwed into place, whereas the other light socket would have been blanked out since its construction.*

Top Left: *Pearson's undertook many different conversions of military vehicles; some were little altered from their original guise, others looked substantially different. For example, this was a Number 11 Cab Chevrolet three-ton 4 x 4 short-wheelbase C60S Model 8442 gasoline tank lorry, but there are conflicting views as to what order it would have originally been supplied on. It is fitted with a tanker body to a design by Thompson Bros (Bilston) Ltd and produced in several factories in Britain and overseas. It appears to be in an 'as withdrawn' state, expect for the 'painted' tyres when it was ready for sale in July 1948.*

Bottom Left: *Whilst many vehicles were not much changed from their war-time role, they looked completely different when pictured in civilian surroundings. The GM DUKW amphibian trucks, seen earlier after testing at Ainsdale, were ideal for holiday-makers' excursion trips. A Southport coach operator, who used Pearson's bodies asked them to supply it with ten DUKW trucks to run tours on the sands of the Lancashire resort, where the local corporation operated a similar service using ex-WD Bedford QL's fitted with passenger seating. Pearson also supplied DUKWs to Blackpool, Morecambe, New Brighton (the one illustrated here) and an operator on the Dee Estuary.*

Below & Right: *This looks to be a 15-cwt 4 x 4 Chevrolet C15A with a front driving axle, which has been given an extreme make-over with a coach-built cab (see the GMC badge) to a cab-over-engine/forward-control tractor. The twin rear wheels indicate that a civilian rear axle has been substituted for the the military one, and the wheels match the trailer's. The front wheels are however military-style with sling flanges. The trailer has a permanently-mounted twin-sectioned fuel tank with two lids. There appears to be a spare single wheel under the rear of the chassis and a vacuum tank behind the cab which powers the trailer brakes.*

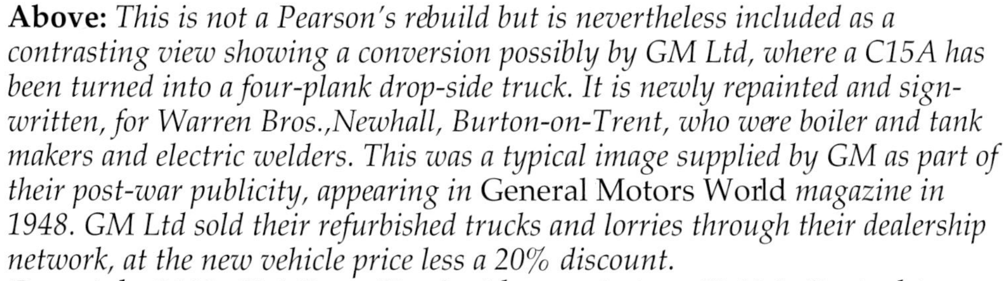

Above: *This is not a Pearson's rebuild but is nevertheless included as a contrasting view showing a conversion possibly by GM Ltd, where a C15A has been turned into a four-plank drop-side truck. It is newly repainted and sign-written, for Warren Bros.,Newhall, Burton-on-Trent, who were boiler and tank makers and electric welders. This was a typical image supplied by GM as part of their post-war publicity, appearing in* General Motors World *magazine in 1948. GM Ltd sold their refurbished trucks and lorries through their dealership network, at the new vehicle price less a 20% discount.*
Copyright 2008. GM Corp. Used with permission. GM Media Archives.

Left: *A large percentage of the vehicles that were refurbished by Pearson's were not intended for general road haulage usage, but rather for the construction and agricultural industries. This photograph, taken in 1945, shows an early re-build job undertaken by Pearson's on a 15-cwt 4 x 4 Chevrolet C15A Number 13 chassis-cab. It has retained the front military wheels and tyres, but gained a civilian-style rear axle with twin wheels, road tyres and new mudguards.*

Top & Bottom Right: *The next two photographs were taken in 1946 and show a similar C15A re-build with EDBRO tipping gear and Pearson body. Note, that in both cases the re-built chassis has been painted gloss black, and this was common with such re-builds by both GM Limited and other authorised dealers.*

Left: *As stated, Pearson's found a good market for their products without the need to fully refurbish them, and these outlets were primarily found in the civil engineering and farming customers. These vehicles did not need to be 'road legal' and quite often were a very basic refurbishment of ex-military units. Adverts were placed in the farming press and the building trade magazines; in these a towing tractor, basically an unaltered Field Artillery Tractor, could be purchased for £175, and these were often used by farmers in place of standard agricultural tractors, which were then in very short supply; a flat bed lorry with one head light and side lights was £195; whilst tippers with hand-operated gear were £250 or £325 with PTO-operated gear. The dearest lorries advertised, fully-converted, in these journals were tarpaulin-covered G/S trucks at £280 plus delivery. These are comparable with prices being offered by Pride & Clarke of South London, who used full-page advertising to sell their wares. the vehicle pictured here is another 1946 photograph of a C15A, with a square roof hatch. In what appears to be a largely un-rebuilt condition with single military wheels and tyres all round, it has new headlamps in both apertures, radiator guard with twin spring leaves, and towing hooks. However, it has been fitted with a metal tipping body with an opening tailgate. This looks to have been the photograph that appeared in a 1946* Builder's Weekly *advert at £250.*

Top Right: *This 1946 photograph shows another C15A, which has an almost identical all-metal tipping body to that shown on the left, but in this case the hydraulic ram can be seen and this is a stark contrast to the tipping gear seen on the previous pages. The bodies here look very similar to a number of larger military tippers that were made by David Brown Fabrications at Salford during World War II, and were fitted to Crossley, Maudslay and AEC chassis. The question is, were these bodies also fitted to the CMPs or are they post-war additions on 'Bitza' trucks. If they are original military bodies, they appear to be remarkably pristine as they do not appear to show any dents or bulges. However, the front wheels are clearly to a military style and they have cross-country tyres, the twin rears are civilian road type on a civilian axle. Both these photographs were taken in 1946.*

Bottom Right: *Again we have another C15A tipper, but this time one with a wooden body of the kind that we know Pearson's produced. No anecdotal evidence has emerged that the firm made welded-steel bodies, although they had the technical capability to do so in the Angela Street plant. Looking at the upper picture on this page, it will also be seen that the welding on the tipper body is very rough in places, whilst the work on the one pictured here is very good, and Pearson's prided themselves on always turning out quality workmanship, even in the height of the war. Observe the radiator guard, tow rings, and single right side blackout headlamp, indicating this as probably being an off-road vehicle. Note it retains military tyres at the front, but has civilian ones at the back.*

Top & Bottom Left: *This pair of photographs is taken on 8th January 1946, at the cleared bomb site off Overbury Street between Spekeland Street and Hulme Street. These are visible (looking in the other direction) in the picture of the Bofors Gun Tractors on pages 14 and 15, whilst the row of houses to the top right of the lorry's tailgate is Albert Terrace, which had a distinctive roof that only sloped to one side of the row of houses. Interestingly, a lot of the broken brickwork from this area was taken into Crown Street railway yards and shipped by rail to East Anglia. Once it arrived at the Whitemoor Marshalling Yards near Peterborough, the rubble was crushed and sent to the sites where new airfields were being built for both the RAF and the USAAF. It is said that when the first operational bombing raids set off from these new airfields, bits of brick from Birmingham, Manchester, Liverpool and London were loaded into the bomb-bays of the aircraft and dropped on targets in Germany, in a case of 'giving them a bit of their own back.' The three-ton Chevrolet C60S lorry pictured here has obviously just come out of the 'Bridge Works' between Angela Street and St. Arnaud Street, and it carries an immaculate all-steel body with hydraulic tipping mechanism. which we conjecture is a post-war production. The elevated body in the upper view allows us to see the spare wheel carrier behind the Number 13 Cab, a new steel box, the military wheels and tyres with flanges on the hubs for slings. The lower view shows us the Chevrolet bow-tie radiator badge, bumper guard, and tow rings. However the driver's side mirror has either not been fitted as yet or has been broken off the stalk! Is it also lacking window glass ahead of the driver?*

Right: *This 1946 photograph, taken by Sefton Park, shows a 30-cwt Chevrolet 4 x 4 C30 Model 8441 chassis with 16" wheels (as against the three-tonners' 20"). It has a similar but longer tipping body to that of the C15As, although obviously longer. the wheels are military style all round without flanges. However the Number 13 Cab has blanked-off headlamp openings and new Lucas headlamps have been mounted in front instead. The radiator brush guard and tow rings have been retained as well on this re-build. We are not quite sure what the original application for this vehicle would have been, but the main chassis members may hold a clue, as these look to have had quite a number of holes drilled into them, which would have been used for mounting something or other. A builder's plate can be seen on the tipper body, but it is just elusive enough to conceal its identity. If any reader can identify the type, we would be very pleased to know what it says.*

Left: *Yet another tipper is pictured in 1946 on the cleared site outside the former works adjacent to the premises of what had been W. E. Wilson & Faquharson Commercial Motor Engineers, Liverpool 7. However, by this time that company's nameplate has been removed from the end gable wall of the building (compare this with the view on page 78). It may be that this garage was located in the Hume Street - Ewart Street area; and the cast-iron sign seen on the wall behind the cab does seem to read Ewart Street. We are also unsure whether this is a Chevrolet C30 (30-cwt) or a C60S (three-ton short wheelbase model) as the cabs were the same. Yet, if you look at the space in between the cab and the wheels, it actually looks like a three-ton cab on a 30-cwt chassis. The cab also provides further questions, such as why the rear window has been reduced in size and then blanked out and painted over, and why have different mudguards been fitted to the refurbished chassis? The tipping body is very unusual, and whilst it looks at first glance to be a manual type, it will be seen that a pipe leads from the cab down to a small reservoir of some kind. It should be noted that on re-builds any differences between the C30 and the C60S could be negated, with replacements of axles, wheels (respectively 16" or 20"), springs and steering components, etc.; resulting in what were commonly referred to as 'Bitza' trucks. Registration evidence suggests that Local Authorities rated the C30 either side of 60-cwts.*

Top Right: *This is again another Chevrolet C30 or a C60S with 16-inch wheels and steel body, but a different hydraulic ram fitted to refurbished chassis. The military wheels have been retained, has as the original No.13 Cab (possibly with the roof hatch removed and plated over). The refurbished and re-painted chassis has new mudguards, and a new tipping body with tailgate has been attached. It will be seen that, like the tipper on the left, the rear cab window has been reduced in size at some stage in its history, but unlike the previous lorry this has not been blanked out in its conversion for civilian use.*

Bottom Right: *Next we have a picture of a Chevrolet 30-cwt C30 with a Number 13 Cab, which has been re-built into a flatbed lorry. The body is made on a frame of steel-angle, whilst a pitch pine bed looks to have been used. Unlike the GM conversion for Warren Bros. Ltd. pictured earlier, this one has been given the luxury of rear mudguards. Even so the cab was, by today's standards very utilitarian; no wonder drivers of those days would go to work wearing ex-army greatcoats, heavy boots and leather gauntlets. The absence of cab windows testify to the fact that driving these in the wintertime was no 'picnic', and as such they were in complete contrast to the sleeper cabs of today with their stylish and comfortable appointment and in-cab entertainment. David Styles recalls that: - "If you wanted entertainment in those days, you had to hum to yourself, and even then you might not even be able to hear yourself above the noise of the engine, gearbox and open road." Note the new headlamps, and the very neat result, albeit some military features have been retained.*

Top Left: *The washed-out Census Number here appears to show 'L 4952929', which is in the C30 batch L 4952859 to 4953033 to Demand S/M 2557 or 2567, for 'Lorry 30-cwt W/T House Arcticized'. Note the Bridge Classification '5' on the left headlamp position, single offside headlamp and the brush guard, etc. These all give the impression of an 'as withdrawn' condition, save that it has been fitted with a brand new metal tipping body, which is similar to that seen on the other tippers shown on the previous pages.*

Bottom Left: *In what was referred to as the Hop Street Yard, in other words right alongside the Phoenix Safe Works (seen in the picture on page 76) we find a Number 13 Cab Chevrolet C30 or C60S. It is fitted with a Canadian Lindsay House-type Wireless body, which has been retained after refurbishment. This may be one of a number of such units that Pearson's sold to the North of Scotland Health Board as travelling medical, X-Ray and dental surgeries for use in rural areas. Aberdeenshire also employed one for use by the Public Health Inspector's Department as an Infestation Control (de-lousing) Centre. The fact that this unit has been painted white suggests that its future use may well have been intended for second use in public health, or even as an ambulance. Indeed, several ambulance services employed ex-CMPs as a stop-gap measure after the war. Note there is no spare wheel behind the cab, nor have the military headlamps been replaced by Lucas or equivalent units. In the background we can just see another former chassis-cab, but cannot make out any further details.*

Right: *We return to the cleared bomb site off Speakland Street once again, where another stunning post-war photograph was taken in 1948. It is a 15-cwt Chevrolet C15A with a Lindsay House-type Wireless body, but this has been designed for a medium-weight truck, and as a consequence the cut-out for the rear wheels does not match up. However, there was a shorter version of this basic body style that abutted the cab and this had the correct wheel cut-out positions. We have not been able to discover if this 'conversion' was a post-war fitting, but the consensus of opinion is that this work was done during the war years when a shortage in chassis supply meant that 15-cwt chassis had to be used in place of the specified models. The truck again looks to be in an 'as acquired' condition; complete with a broken right headlamp and military wheels with flanges. However, new sidelights have been fitted and they stand out in stark contrast to the rest of the weather-worn body. It will also be noted that a further body has been removed from another chassis and sits grounded to the rear of the CMP, suggesting that this vehicle may be awaiting the same fate?*

Left: *A series of views were taken in June 1946 at Sefton Park of another Chevrolet 30-cwt C30 with a House-Type body and heater. This one shows the rear tent that could be erected at the rear of the truck. However it lacks a wiper blade on the driver's side! These photographs show that this was a high-quality re-build with grommets for wiring, and as there is a tax disc, it must have been intended for civilian use; perhaps as a Dentist's surgery or for the National Fire Service, especially as it retains the military tyres.*

Top & Bottom Right: *These two views show the front and rear of i.e. 'Lorry 30-cwt 4 x 4 Office', which may have originally been 'Winterised' as there are two fuel tanks. At the front, the headlamps have been replaced by Lucas units post-war and the new spare tyre is mounted under the rear of the body. The tank on the roof appears to have been fabricated from aluminium or thin-gauge steel and is evidently for water.*

Below: *An interior view showing the quality of the workmanship, with lighting and heating, and a tap fed from the roof-mounted tank.*

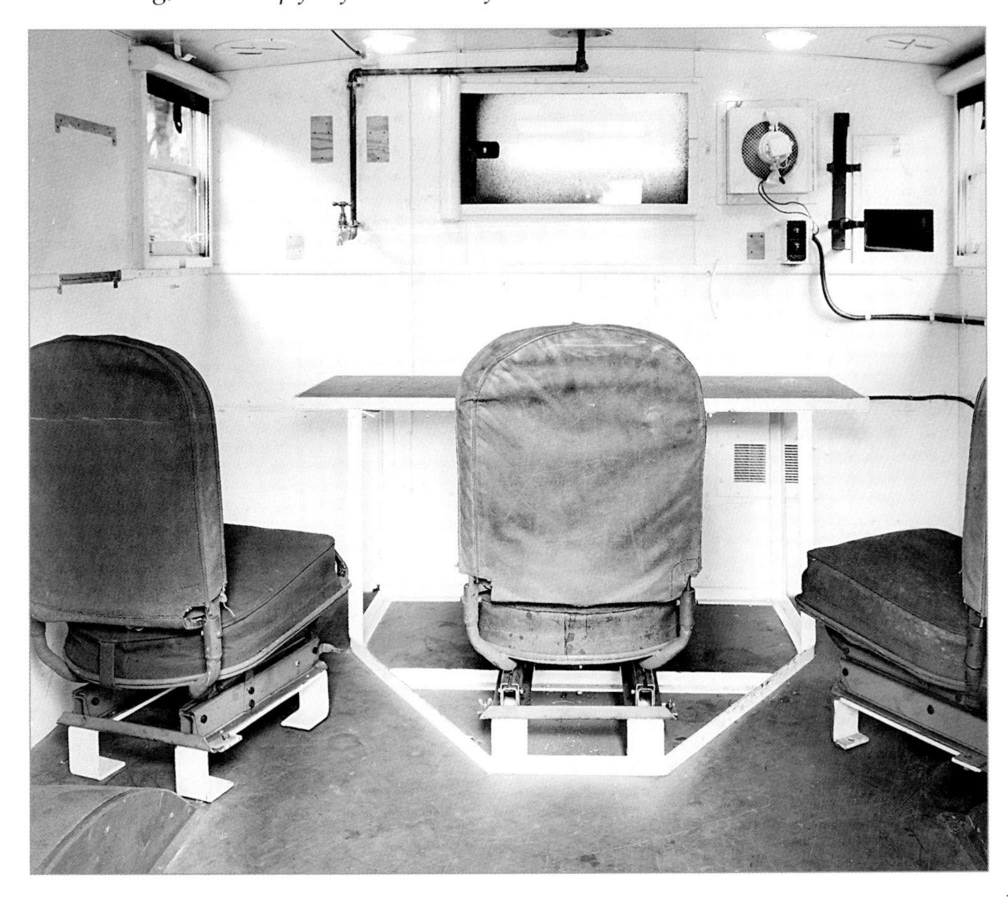

Top Left: *This is another view of the Number 13 Cab 15-cwt 4 x 4 Chevrolet C15A (shown on page 99, bottom left), converted to a fifth-wheel tractor. It has an unusual body, which has been made from reclaimed packing case timbers. If you look at the end board of the trailer, you will see that it has vertical planks for one-third of the length on the off-side, and horizontal planks for the remaining two thirds, showing that the timber was only available in restricted lengths. The wooden-body on the semi-trailer used three-ton military rear wheels on a straight axle, and Allun Armstrong recalls: "The firm used to deal with a company called Eaton for supplies, which were brought by railway from the Bolton area." The cab has the square type roof hatch, military tow rings, and radiator brush guard. Note that replacement Lucas headlamps have been fitted and the original headlamp holes plated over, whilst new side lamps have also been added. Sadly the back end of the trailer has been cropped off in the picture when the negative was printed in 1946. The stencilled number RS 387 on the front bumper would not correspond with the usual chalked R/S mark (which stood for Repair or Salvage) and it is therefore something of a puzzle, and various suggestions have been put forward. From pencilled comments on the back of one print in the collection, we know that a similar stencilled RS number referred to it as being an ex-Royal Signals Corps vehicle.*

Bottom Left: *This is yet another 'refurbished' CMP that has obviously been given a 'Heath Robinson' type body by the Pearson's workmen. It appears to have been made out of re-cycled packing crates, and is fitted to a 'General Motors' three-ton C60X Model 8660 (actually a Chevrolet 6 x 6 chassis). The (probably) ex-Canadian lorry seen here is otherwise largely untouched, and having been given 'road-legal' lighting is ready for work. The engine on this was not the same as the majority of GM CMPs (216 cubic-inch Chevrolet six-cylinder) but was a US-built GMC 270 cu in 'six' similar to that used in the armoured CMP derivatives. It is pictured outside the Angela Street or 'Bridge Works in May 1947.*

Right: *At the junction of Queensland Street and Smithdown Lane, with Albert Terrace behind, we see a Diamond T Model 967 on 8th January 1946. This one has the closed cab, and has a full canvas tilt to the back. Behind it and to the left can be seen an open cab Diamond T 969 Wrecker with Gar Wood crane. The chalk marks under the front wing suggest that it is being handled under a Ministry of Supply contract, as a number of these lorries were converted for 'essential users' in the post-war period and allocated by the MoS. If this truck was originally supplied to a British order, rather than a Canadian one, then it may well have been supplied to Demand S/M 2591, L 5475928 to 5476127.*

M.O.S.

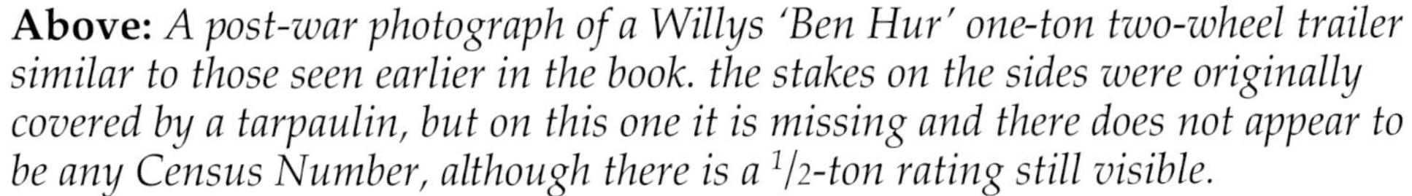

Above: *A post-war photograph of a Willys 'Ben Hur' one-ton two-wheel trailer similar to those seen earlier in the book. the stakes on the sides were originally covered by a tarpaulin, but on this one it is missing and there does not appear to be any Census Number, although there is a $^{1}/_{2}$-ton rating still visible.*

Left: *This fascinating photograph is another taken in one of the Pearson compounds off (perhaps the Gravel Yard?), although we are not really sure which one. Perhaps the painter and decorator's shop in the background will serve as a clue to some readers. The vehicle is a re-built 15-cwt 4 x 4 US-sourced Dodge WC.56 Command Car (no winch appears to have been fitted in the front). If this was a British order then it would have been to Demand S/M 2584, Census Numbers Z 4577078 to 4577107, 'Truck 10-cwt 4 x 4 Command Recce', Model T-214-B-98.*

Top Right and Bottom Right: *This trailer looks like a standard Trailer two-ton four-wheeled dropside minus its sides and tail-board. These trailers were made by various makers in both the UK and Canada to a basically similar pattern. A large number of these were sold to farmers and other agricultural users post-war; look in any issue of one of the agricultural journals of the period (e.g.:* Farmer's Weekly*) and you will find at least four or five adverts from different dealers who were offering such trailers for sale.*

The next collection of pictures of the Leyland Super-Beaver and Super Hippo models intrigued the Leyland Society so much, that Neil Steele spent several hours in his personal archive looking for an article about these vehicles and eventually found that the Super Beaver appeared on page 66 of *Leyland Journal* Vol.8 No.2, March 1948, with notes that read: -

"A special cab designed to give comfort and protection equally in conditions of excessive heat and excessive cold is now being offered by Leyland Motors Ltd. It is intended for use on Leyland heavy export goods chassis, which are of the bonneted type, and is built by Pearson's of Liverpool, who designed it in conjunction with Leyland engineers. A double skin is used throughout, and in it is sandwiched Isoflex insulating material, a corrugated plastic-type paper built up of laminations. As an additional shield against the direct rays of the sun, there is a detectable sun-shade panel over the roof. A visor runs the full length of the windscreen.

Stress on the cab when the chassis beneath it is weaving or flexing over rough country is reduced by three-point flexible mounting. Two mounting points at the front of the cab bear directly on the chassis frame, but the third attachment is positioned centrally at the back and is pivoted to a truss bar; this bar runs transversely behind the cab and bears on rubber pads carried in brackets that are attached to the chassis frame members. A 4-seater extends the full width of the cab. Beneath it are three compartments, the centre one containing the batteries and the other two being intended for personal kit. The complete cab is designed to match the chassis in its capacity for withstanding tough overseas operating conditions."

Neil considered that these pictures were taken in 1948, as in later *Leyland Journals* the extent of this contract became clear. Commenting "LM Ltd. procured an order for 400 vehicles from the Anglo Iranian Oil Co. Some 268 vehicles of this order were for Super Beaver & Super Hippo tankers, the tanks being built by Butterfield of Shipley, Thompson Bros. (Bilston) Ltd. and the Steel Barrel Co. Uxbridge." He concludes:-

"It would appear that Leyland's association with Pearson's was short-lived as in July 1949 a new design of cab for the 'Super' range was announced, initially being built 'in-house'."

Top Left: *Left-hand drive Leyland Super Beaver 6 x 4 ten-wheel rigid chassis cab, note the supports that would hold the back of the tanker body.*

Bottom Left: *By contrast this is a left-hand drive Leyland Super Beaver tractor unit.*

Right: *Another shot inside the 'Bridge Works' on Angela Street, with several Leyland Hippo export models seen being completed as chassis-cabs, with what appears to be roof racks mounted on the top of the insulated cabs.*

WAITING ROOM
LEYLAND
Hippo

Top Left: *A frontal view of the Leyland Super Beaver 4 x 2 chassis-cab. Note that there is only a sole driver's side mirror.*

Bottom Left: *Another view, this time showing the profile of the Leyland Super Beaver three-ton 4 x 2 chassis-cab. This view reveals the position of the exhaust pipe/silencer and spare wheel at the rear overhang.*

Below: *A reproduction of an article on Pearson's that appeared in the* Commercial Motor *magazine during 1946, and was thereafter re-printed and used as an advertising poster by the company until about 1949.*

A few of the 32,000 Service machines of many varied types dealt with by Messrs. Pearson's, of Liverpool, since they started assembly work in 1940. Every available inch of space surrounding the depot was utilised for parking and convoy purposes.

Northern Distributors Fine War Job

Liverpool firm puts through a grand total of 32,000 Service Vehicles in Four Year's effort.

DAY by day stories are being released dealing with the splendid work which has been carried out by various sections of the motor industry; here is one which deals with the activities, during the war period, of a northern distributor—Messrs. Pearson's, of Shaw Street, Liverpool.

It starts with the acquisition in December, 1940, of a much-bombed and derelict factory building in Smithdown Lane, the total area being approximately 100,000 sq. ft. The first assembly line and lifting gear for the erection of imported vehicles was installed at the Shaw Street premises of the firm, but the demand became so heavy that assembly work had to be extended to the newly acquired roofless factory in Smithdown Lane. This was late in February, 1941, at a time when roofing operations were actually going on, but enthusiasm on the part of all concerned overcame all difficulties, including the worst possible climatic conditions.

The lifting of cases weighing anything between 4½ and 13½ tons was carried out with manually operated tackle installed to meet the emergency.

In May, 1941, enemy action caused further considerable damage to the premises and reconstruction work, but assembly did not stop, and by July in the same year the firm were turning out on the Smithdown Lane assembly line one [illegible] lorry every 20 minutes, the work including the carrying out of from 30 to 40 modifications.

By August, considerable extensions had been carried out to meet the requirements of the Canadian Forces, and by May, 1942, there came the demands of the American Armies. At this period, more than 100,000 sq. ft. of floor space was occupied in assembly work, the overflow, in the form of parking places, extending around the whole area of the plant.

All the time progress was being made in the way of improvements in equipment, high-speed [illegible] and pneumatic tools being introduced to quicken assembly work; electric cranes and hoists were provided at points where required and, in other ways, the build-up was such as to make the premises into a first-class vehicle assembly depot.

To meet the requirements of supply to the assembly lines, and to accommodate the parking areas containing "broken-down" vehicles, 15 acres of storage space were operated a few miles from Liverpool. At the peak period the value of the vehicles contained in this storage area exceeded £4,000,000.

Many types of load carrier and other vehicles have been dealt with, from the ubiquitous jeep to 10-ton tractors and Tank-transporter trailers. Prior to D-day, an average of 30 to 40 different types of machines were being dealt with at one time, together with large numbers of amphibious load carriers, armoured scout cars and half-track vehicles. The peak output per week averaged about 120 machines, with a grand total of no fewer than 32,000.

This, we feel, is a splendid effort, for it must be remembered that the labour employed was, for the most part, unskilled and had to be trained on the job.

Another imposing view of left-hand drive Leyland Super Beaver fitted with the special Leyland-designed cab that was built by Pearson & Co. in Smithdown Road, Liverpool. As an additional shield against the direct rays of the desert sun that would be encountered in Iran, there is a detachable sun-shade panel over the roof, whilst a visor runs the full length of the windscreen.

Left: *One of the least common types to be refurbished by Pearson during the post-war era were the Southall-built products of AEC. Whilst AEC bus chassis were regularly bodied or re-bodied by the company, both before the war and afterwards, AEC commercial vehicle applications were few and far between. However, after a disposal sale held at Speke in January 1948, Pearson's purchased about 30 aircraft refuelling tankers on AEC chassis. These were the AEC model 854 (with petrol engines) or O854 (with oil/diesel units). Developed from the Matador 'Tractor 4 x 4 Medium', these tankers were introduced when the RAF went over to the Wellington and Lancaster types. A fully-fuelled Lancaster needed 2,146 gallons of aviation spirit, and the tankers that had to deliver this needed to be capable of cross-country traction.*

This Page: *This 10-ton tanker was fitted with a semi-elliptical stainless-steel body with a capacity of 2,500 gallons, which had four separate compartments or one single one. An added feature of this model was the two-speed Turner power winch capable of pulling seven tons, thus making it capable of aircraft recovery or towing. The AEC tankers purchased by Pearson's were available with either petrol or diesel engines and most were delivered during February and March 1948. Several were refurbished as chemical tankers, with purchasers including Bootle Transport, La Porte Chemicals, Liverpool Corporation (Airports), The Pink Paraffin Co, Ringway Airport (Manchester), Suttons and others.*

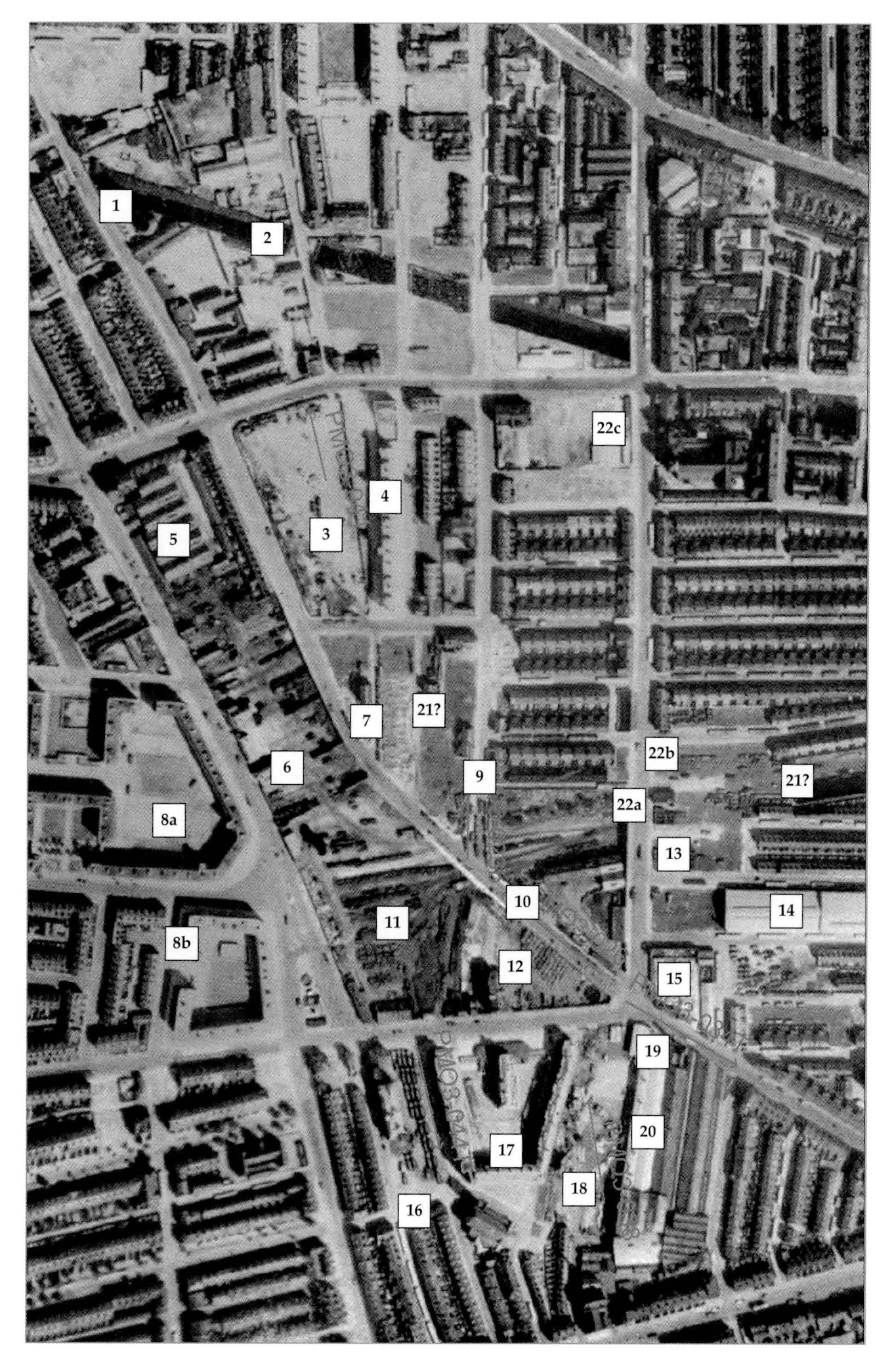

Left: *This superb 1945 aerial view has proved most useful in showing the area where Pearson's operations were centred as it shows the bomb-damaged streets, with whole rows of houses being decimated in the areas around the railway yards and tunnels [1]. With good eyesight and possibly a magnifying glass, you can also pick out the Corporation Stables and Ramsbottom's Chimney [2]. To the west of this is the Gravel Yard [3], a triangular site near Sidney Gardens [4], which was used as a secure compound until 1946. Concentrations of vehicles are also seen in Queensland Street [9], the Smithdown Lane Compound [10], the despatch area at Oliver Street by the Windsor Sugar Mills [16], and around the factory on Angela Street [13 & 14]. In these you can pick out traces of Pearson's ongoing activity. A large number of Jeeps are seen in the Crown Street Goods Yard, just to the right of the figure 12. By contrast the storage yards at 165, Smithdown Lane [7], Myrtle Gardens/Myrtle House/ Almond Gardens [8] and Windsor Gardens [17] are either completely empty or have only a few isolated vehicles or packing cases left within them. Looking at the yards alongside the Phoenix Safe Works [19 & 20] shows that work has drastically slowed down at this stage. The large storage compound on Smithdown Lane [10], from its junction with Overbury street and Falkner Street and leading up to Cardwell Street only has a few vehicles within it.*

The locations that are identified by numbers in boxes are as follows: -

1. *Liverpool Corporation's Central Stables & Ramsbottom's Chimney;*
2. *Lime Street railway cutting and tunnel portal;*
3. *The 'Gravel Yard' compound;*
4. *The Sidney Gardens Tenements;*
5. *The LMS Railway Agricultural Warehouse;*
6. *The old Crown Street passenger station;*
7. *The remains of the original works at 165, Smithdown Lane;*
8. *The Myrtle Gardens/Myrtle House Tenements storage area.*
9. *Queensland Street Storage Area;*
10. *Smithdown Lane Secure Compound;*
11. *Crown Street Railway Goods & Coal Yards;*
12. *Crown Street Railway Goods Yard vehicle dismantling area;*
13. *The Speakland Street – Hume Street vehicle storage area;*
14. *Pearson's Bridge Works, Angela Street;*
15. *The Mersey Marble Works;*
16. *The Oliver Street vehicle despatch area;*
17. *The Windsor Gardens Tenements crating area;*
18. *The Hop Street Yard, vehicle un-crating facility;*
19. *The original Phoenix Safe Works;*
20. *The Phoenix Works Extension;*

21? *Possible sites of W. E. Wilson & Farquarson, Motor Engineers;*

22. *Queensland Street Dumps (at least three).*

Evidently Pearson's refurbished this Bedford ML code 55, possibly a 'three-ton 4 x 2 Petrol', which dates from 1940 as shown by the original Willenhall cab and radiator. They also re-built 'flat front' (former military or WD) Bedford lorries such as OY, OYC, OYD and OWLD to passenger-carrying vehicles as well as wartime utility OWB buses with a similar front end to the WL, which was pictured in March 1947.

Both Pages: *Pearson's, like many other British industries, experienced a large programme of re-equipment immediately after World War II, as the country struggled to re-build itself. This was also a time when the need for public transport was increasing due to the fact that the production of new cars was strictly limited. Obviously this made great demands on the bus operators as people needed to travel too and from work, but the problem was further compounded by the fact that as people began to take interest in leisure activities, day excursions and holidays were essential to a nation recovering from the ravages of a six-year-long war. Relatively few comfortable coaches had survived the war years, and those that did needed major overhauls. The solution was the complete refurbishment of some former service buses into coaches, especially the rather spartan OWBs; the only single-deck service buses to be built during the war years. The OWB bodies were only ever intended as being a 'short-term' solution, and hundreds of them were falling to bits by the time the war ended. As a result Pearson's began re-bodying large batches of OWBs, as well as new chassis by Austin, Bedford and Commer. These photographs show new bodies being built, ready for fitting on to both wartime Bedford OWB and post-war OB chassis, whilst on the right of the factory are several brand new Leyland Beaver chassis, including one with a tanker body. At this date Pearson's were still officially registered at 168, Smithdown Lane, Liverpool 8, but the Body Building Section was by 1949 recorded as being at 182, Smithdown Lane.*

Left: *These views show what appears to be a 1945 Bedford OB, however this vehicle had a far from simple life for its chassis was sent to Pearson's for 'Prototype Bodying' in 1939, but was then 'frozen' when PSV production was halted for the duration of the war. Many of the parts were stripped from this vehicle until it was down to just the frame, however it was eventually re-built in the early post-war period. It is seen with Liverpool trade plates (321 LV), whilst undergoing the tilt test for Ministry of Transport approval prior to being sent to Luton for bodywork 'Type Approval'.*

Below: *An interior shot taken of the coach in Sefton Park showing the very high quality of the finished coachwork of the Pearson-bodied Bedford OB, note the use of the attractive moquette and leather.*

Right: *This is a photograph of it in Sunniways livery, which was taken outside the Vauxhall showroom at Luton in July 1945 during the 'Type Approval' process. Pearson's traded as both Happy Days Motor Ways and Sunniways, which were incorporated as Pearson's of Liverpool Ltd. in 1950. They ran amongst other vehicles, two Pearson-bodied OBs, plus ex-WD OY and OYD lorries, and a Leyland Tiger TS1, all acquired 1947-9.*

MONDAYS TO FRIDA
TO OPEN
OFF

ALEXANDRE
TAILOR
HALFORDS
CYCLE & MOTOR STORES
MEESON
PRIVATE
Sunniways
COACHWAYS
KKA 263

Left: *Another post-war rebuild, but this time it is on an ex-army OY lorry chassis, which was operated by Pearson's under their Sunniways trade name and possibly painted yellow. This OY chassis number 78405 (1944) was bodied with a C28F body and carries a late-21948 or early-1949 registration mark (KKA 263). Note will be made that this street scene was photographed at a time when almost everyone wore a hat, although the Meeson's store is obviously well patronised, there are other familiar well-known shops in the locality such as Alexandre the Tailor and Halford's cycle and motor stores. As for the Bedford, it is not surprising to state that they had a slogan 'You see then everywhere.'*

Top Right: *Many bus and coach operators who had examples of the Bedford OWB, which were quite utilitarian in their 'bus' format with wooden-slatted seats, had them re-seated in leather or moquette. Others had internal refurbishment and alteration of the 'squared' front roof dome, which made them look a lot less frugal in their appointments. Yet other companies found that as the chassis were very sound, it made practical and economical common sense to have a new body fitted. Many curious designs of bodywork were consequently fitted to newly-overhauled Bedford OWB chassis in the post-war years, perhaps the strangest was a half-cab forward-control by Willenhall. Another post-war re-build of a Bedford OWB was this example with a conventional composite coachwork constructed by Pearson's. The vehicle seen here at Sefton Park was only waiting the flourish of the sign-writer's artwork and the fitting of the destination blinds.*

Bottom Right: *This Bedford OWB is the same coach as that in the photograph above, but is taken after all the lettering had been applied. This Pearson-bodied coach was obviously supplied to Watson of Winsford, although no mention of it can be found in the records that have survived to this day. The operator did have a 1945 B32F OWB bodied by Duple, which was withdrawn in 1956, and it was suggested by one bus historian that this was a post-war rebuild on that chassis with C26F body! However, given the date of these photographs in November 1946, this does not seem likely. The registration plate dates from 1947, and it is undoubtedly a re-built OWB. These models were the wartime equivalent of the OB chassis and although bodied by various concerns, such as Roe, Duple and SMT all of which were fitted with the same style of B32F utility bodies to a MoS stringent and very basic design. However even on the re-bodied examples, such as this one, a point of difference between the OWB and the OB models is seen with the positioning of the headlights; the OWB models had them mounted at a higher position than the Bedford OB models.*

Both Pages: *This Bedford OB (registration JTU 888), chassis number 57031, had a Pearson's C26F coach body and was registered by Cheshire County Council in November 1947. The coach was also registered to Watsons (Winsford Motor Services Ltd of Stonefield Garage, 67 High Street, Winsford, Cheshire). It was later sold to H B Clague of Douglas, Isle of Man and re-registered KMN 854. Watson apparently had several Bedford WTB coaches from 1938 onwards, and amongst other post-war vehicles, a Pearson-bodied C28F Austin CXB registration KTU 11, Chassis Number 122541, which was new in February 1949. These views of the Bedford OB were again taken at Sefton Park, a location that appears in many of the Pearson publicity images. The view clearly emphasises the difference in height of the headlights on the Bedford OB, especially if these are compared with the OWB models pictured earlier. To explain these differences look at the centre of the headlight on the Bedford OB, seen here, and this will be observed to be on par with the second chrome bar of the radiator grille. The OWB's lights, being by necessity fitted with the war-time black-out masks, were built with headlights on a slightly higher plane to give a longer range. The OB was one of the most successful buses/coaches of all time, and one wonders just how many would have been produced had normal production not been disrupted from just after its inception in 1939, and the end of the war in 1945?*

Watsons
Watsons
JTU 888

PRIVATE
HUNT'S
JTC 568
COACHWORK by
Pearsons of Liverpo

Left & Right: *This series of official photographs show an Austin CXB Chassis Number 103897, which was bodied by Pearson's with a C28F coach body. It was supplied to, and registered by A & W Hunt (Robert Hunt & Sons) of 3, Rainford Road, Bickerstaff, Lancashire in March 1948. The CXB might best be considered as Austin's answer to the famous Bedford OB, but whilst large numbers were built, the model was never a serious contender for Luton's crown. Often called the 'Birmingham Bedford', the CXB was introduced in 1947 as Austin's post-war coach chassis. The Austin models were normal-control chassis and designed for a 29–seat coach body and had a wheelbase of 15'. The chassis were initially fitted with an Austin six cylinder 3.5-litre ohv petrol engine. However, whereas the OB and OWB had a non-synchro four-speed 'crash' gearbox, the Longbridge equivalent reputedly had a much superior drive train with synchromesh on all four gears. The brakes were of the Lockheed hydraulic type. In 1948 the engine was up rated to four-litres. Incidentally, this very coach was featured in the* Commercial Motor, *which carried advertisements from Pearson's in the summer of 1948.*

Below: *Here we have the interior of the Hunt's coach showing the quality of the workmanship in its appointments, making quite a luxury coach on what was a very modestly-priced vehicle. This was another example of Pearson bodywork with a sliding sunroof, an option that many operators stipulated in the carefree and easy (pre-motorway years) in order to allow their passengers to take full advantage of the glorious warm summer weather. This coach was apparently still in service in 1961, albeit with a different operator.*

Top Left: *Seen in Angela Street (un-officially known as the Bridge Works) is an oil-engined AEC Regal Mk III, Chassis Number O6625665, bodied by Pearson's with a C33F luxury body. On completion it was acquired by MacShanes Commercial Motors Ltd, 46 St Johns Lane, Liverpool 1 having been painted Ivory/Red, and registered JKD 58 in July 1948. They subsequently acquired several Duple- and a Harrington-bodied Regals, however. It was later sold to Bee Jay Coachways Ltd of Warrington in April 1954, who also bought DBU 146, chassis O6624664 (Plaxton C33F body), though they went into receivership in February 1956*

Bottom Left: *A rear three-quarter view of JKD 58, which was featured in an advertisement in the* Commercial Motor *on 26th November 1948; from which we see that the print has had the operator's name obscured from the glass panel below the rear window ventilation system. The body four central bays, and an emergency exit just behind the driver's door. A typical feature of many touring coaches that were built by Pearson's around this time was once again the inclusion of a sliding sunroof; this can just be seen above the two leading bays of the bodywork. The touring coaches at that time were obligated to run at less than half the speed of today's motorway coaches and comfort was of prime importance when passengers might be aboard the vehicle for a long time between rest stops.*

Right: *Another series of official photographs shows a Leyland PS1/1, registered JP 6412, carrying a similar body style to that seen on the AEC. It had chassis number 470488 and a Pearson's C33F body, which was new to Smiths of Wigan in 1948/1949. This picture clearly shows the elegant body design, but it will be observed that it carries an alternate design of side flash from the AEC Regal, whilst front entrance is via a sliding door. After three years in front-line service with Smith's it was sold to Wilfred Morris; this firm also operated a Leyland PS1/1JP 6411, and JP 6413, a PS1/1 Chassis Number 470486 each of which had an almost identical body from Webster of Wigan. At this time, Smith's (as a general rule) only kept their coaches for no more than five years, as there was a high demand and a corresponding high price for second-hand AEC and Leyland coaches with quality bodies. However, Smiths' also refurbished a number of their coach chassis and had the bodies re-built, quite often with full front cabs rather than half-cabs. Ostensibly emerging as new vehicles, these re-builds were good for a further three or four years service.*

SWITZERLAND
SMITH'S
LEYLAND
35
JP 6412
COACHWORK
by
Pearsons of Liverpool

Above: *Here we have a near-side view showing the bodywork on JP 6412, which was quite clearly a quality product. Allun Armstrong also recalls: - "The factory was a double storey building, but only one floor was in use; the whole left-hand side was the stores, on the right was the paint shop and the middle section was where they built the coaches and reconditioned some military vehicles. There were always three or four coaches under construction and at the far end of the main floor there was a 'body shop', which really fascinated me because the body-builders would take a flat sheet of metal then, by beating it with different hammers, they would produce perfect mudguards, bonnets, boot lids in fact they produced all the bodywork.... Those men were skilled".*

Bottom Left: *This interior view shows a different window arrangement on a Pearson body for another Smith's Leyland, and is possibly that fitted to JP 6411. The distinctive rear window design that was fitted to some of Pearson's bodies, was similar in design to those seen on Harrington coach bodies with a 'Dorsal Fin' style that incorporated the internal ventilation system. This photograph clearly shows the luxurious interior, where the leather-trimmed seats are finished in a ' a woollen velour moquette by Holdsworth of Halifax'.*

Top Right: *One of the refurbished coaches (JP 6412) was originally bodied similar to JP 7221 in 1948, but was then re-built and converted to forward-control by Pearson's in 1949 with a new C33F body. The conversion of traditional buses and coaches to full-front coachwork was often nothing more than a fashion whim. The demise of the half-cab was really brought about by the introduction of the various under-floor engine PSV chassis at the beginning of the 1950s, which made relatively new coaches look 'old-fashioned' overnight. In a fickle material world, where the consumer always wanted the latest and most up-to-date gimmick, coach proprietors like Smith's would often choose to have a half-cab coach re-built to full-front specification. The coach owner who chose to have a coach altered to a full-front layout often benefited from a travelling public who convinced themselves that they were going away to a holiday destination on a new vehicle. The only problem anyone seemed to have had in building full-front bodies, was what they would then do with the front end appearance once they had concealed the radiator grille, which up till then had been the focal point; hence the heavy usage of chrome rubbing strips as seen here.*

Bottom Right: *The lower picture shows the front end interior of JP 6412, clearly illustrating the handrail for the steps to the left, whilst on the opposite side of the engine cowl is the driver's position; this arrangement obviously provided the driver with a less claustrophobic cabin, however the area to the left of the driver serves little purpose. Regretfully, with the engine remaining in the position that it occupied, the area to the left of the driver could not be used as additional seating unlike that on a new under-floor engine coach. Furthermore, the exercise often led to a more time consuming labour period for the fitter, for although the front panel was removable (after undoing about a dozen screws) it did not allow the fitter the same freedom as a removable side panel and bonnet. Wigan folk remember the firm of Smith's with great affection. For example, one of the town's more famous sons, the actor Ian McKellen, had fond memories of the late 1940s, especially as his father had been promoted to the post of Borough Engineer in 1949. With increased affluence, and living across the road from Mesnes Park, the comings and goings of the Smith's buses were common sights in his childhood. He wrote of his nostalgia in the* Sunday Times Magazine *on 2nd January 1977:- "On the same Market Place in summer, Smith's coaches prepared for the Lake District, North Wales, London and even the Continent. I imagined as they waited to leave, full of locals in best hats and Sunday suits, that the buses had newly arrived whence they were going. And I paraded up and down them, proud to belong to Wigan, tourist attraction and centre of the world." Not everyone liked Smith's however, for in August 1949, the Ministry of Town & Country Planning held an enquiry at the Town Hall into Wigan Corporation's refusal to permit Messrs. Smith & Co. Ltd., motor coach proprietors, to erect an advertisement 30' high on the elevation of their premises in Market Street, opposite Market Square.*

Top Left: *This photograph illustrates a typical half-cab coach with Pearson bodywork in profile, showing a design intended for popular chassis of that time such as the Leyland Tiger, AEC Regal or Maudslay Marathon. All of these well-respected vehicles were among the most popular choices of chassis for bus and coach operators who were looking for a quality product rather than opting for the smaller, more economical Austin, Bedford or Commer types. The design featured neat sculptured styling to the skirt and the rear end, and deep wrap-around rear fenders, which were at the time rather reminiscent of the Thomas Harrington products. The slim, polished window pillars with the glass louvres above were all among the typical styling features to be found on many of the British touring coaches during the early post-war period. The sweep of the wheel arch trims and the painted side-flash were also typical styling features on the majority of British coach-builders of the late 1940s and early 1950s period with a great many different interpretation's carried out by all the leading and many of the minor coach body builders.*

Bottom Left: *Pearson's bodied various PSV chassis, including several double-deckers for various undertakings; Liverpool Corporation being just one example. However, they seem to have handled more Bedford chassis than any other, which is perhaps not surprising considering the firm's association with General Motors, the owners of first Vauxhall Motors and then Bedford. Yet, in their advert, they proudly proclaimed that they specialised in 'Coach Body Production on Bedford, Austin, Commer, Leyland, AEC Single & Double Deck Service Bodies.' The coach in this official photograph is a 33-seat Commer Avenger, the body for which has been constructed with a sliding door that is set further back than on some of the previous designs. This resulted with the bodywork being designed with a complimentary short off-side bay of equal width opposite the door. This coach, which was in the fleet of Taylor's was another vehicle that was featured in a* Commercial Motor *advertisement in May 1950. Interestingly, this body incorporated a different style of window frame arrangement, which consisted of the main framework member with alternate bright pillars giving a panoramic effect. The side trim was also new, but had rather simple brightwork following the curve of the waist rail. Furthermore, the design lost the graceful sweep of the rear wheel arch trim too, as this was replaced with a design that finished with a sudden fall at the rear rather than continue the sweep into the rear-end lower body roll.*

Top Right: *Initially, this forward-control FC24F bodied coach was a mystery vehicle, and not found in the order book pages that survived; though a page from 1948 was missing. It was however registered UHX 711, which was a London 1948 number, so that confirmed the build date. The 'Motorway' company blind the made ownership identification difficult. Yet, by electronic photo-enhancement we have been able to read the legal lettering; this tells us that the coach was operated by F. Thomsett, Manager, Valiant Direct Coach Services, Ealing. Chris Taylor of the Historic Commercial Vehicle Society thus identified it as a Regal MkIII (chassis no. 9621A678). He also notes that the company had another Pearson-bodied coach, this time a FC30F (VME 172), which was built on an AEC Regal MkIII chassis (chassis no. 9621A744). We then found out that UHX 711 travelled from the Liverpool works to appear in the 1948 Commercial Motor show and also featured in a* Commercial Motor *advert placed by Pearson's in 1949. The body design used here was very similar to the one Pearson's used for their half-cab coaches, with only the cab front being really dissimilar. Looking inside the cabin, you can see that there was a glazed, full-height bulkhead behind the driver. The front panel of the coach follows the same practice of many coachbuilders of the day, especially as they came to convert traditional coaches to full front variants. Having concealed the manufacturer's distinctive exposed radiator, they often incorporated into the body a rather nondescript or plain front panel. This was then finished off along with the front of the bodywork with the application of bands of brightwork.*

Bottom Right: *One of the most popular of all British coach chassis particularly among the small private operator was the Bedford OB, which had been introduced in 1939. Although Pearson's became appointed as an 'approved body-builder', the example that was sent from Luton was never bodied as only 73 OBs were manufactured before production was halted for the war. As stated earlier, the chassis was re-introduced during 1945 and continued in production until 1951, during which time 12,766 examples were built. As so many were constructed with the very well known Duple Vista bodywork it is often overlooked that many other coach builders clothed the chassis too. These were in the main normal control examples but others were built as full front forward control. The vehicle illustrated here is of a 31-seater luxury coach and a photograph of the same vehicle appeared in a* Commercial Motor *advertisement in October 1949. This shows a forward-control conversion of what is (by consensus of opinion) believed to be a Bedford OB chassis, although Pearson's did body a variety of different chassis makes.*

Top & Bottom Left: *The luxurious interiors of these Pearson coaches were furnished by using a choice of woollen worsted moquette patterns by Holdsworth of Halifax for the seat upholstery, which were fitted on the Dean seat frames. The floor and inspection hatches (one of them being open in the upper photograph), being covered with hard-wearing and waterproof materials that were supplied by Dunlop. The majority of coachbuilders during that time, where possible, aimed to incorporate various styling whims and give coach operators as much choice as possible. Note will be made of the interior in the upper photograph and the way that the ceiling is finished to bring a certain harmony to the division of the twin rear windows. While the coach in the lower photograph has been built with a one-piece rear screen and the ceiling is again styled accordingly. The interiors differ further by such features as the luggage racks above the passenger seats and the individual treatment of their seat lighting; in one view, the interior lighting is situated beneath the luggage racks while the vehicle in the other view has perpendicular opaque lights set against the window pillars.*

Right: *Another Austin CXB with a Pearson C26F coach body, newly-delivered to Rosslyn. It was featured in a* Commercial Motor *advertisement of 2nd September 1949. On many of the Pearson bodies, such as the one here fitted to an Austin chassis, the window pillars featured neat radii at the bottom corners. While at the top of the bay they were fitted with these discrete glass louvres, or alternate full length steel ones. This style of Pearson body was virtually identical to those, which were also designed and fitted to the Bedford OB and Commer Q4 models.*

With these images, we come to a conclusion of a ten-year period in the history of an interesting, if not unique, company that played a vital war-time and immediate post-war role in the motor vehicle history of the British Isles. Few people will have hitherto appreciated precisely what this company did, and the role they played in the dark days of World War II. The extent of their operations and the size of their compounds in the Wavertree and Edge Hill areas has long been forgotten, and the painful destruction of the same districts by Hitler's Luftwaffe have almost thankfully faded from living memory. However, amidst all this turmoil and destruction, the Pearson operation struggled to raise from the ashes, to begin a vehicle assembly operation that was a pivotal point in the later Allied offensive; perhaps there is no small coincidence in the fact that the main centre for their operations was based in the former Phoenix Safe Works!

ROSSLYN
Rosslyn
GSP 300

With a book of this nature, it is impossible to know how to acknowledge all the people who have willingly contributed assistance towards it, but to them we offer our sincere thanks. We are particularly appreciative of the extensive help received from: The AEC Society, Allun Armstrong, John Bates, Robert Berry, David Bracksome, Dave Brison, The Canadian War Museum, Canadian Military Vehicle Forum, Caterpillar Inc., David Fletcher, Ford Motors, General Motors, Les Freathy, David Haigh, The Imperial War Museum, The Leyland Society, The *Liverpool Echo*, Liverpool Museums, Liverpool Record Office, Mack Trucks Inc, 'Maple Leaf Up', Neil Steele, The Tank Museum Bovington, Chris Taylor, Mike Sutcliffe, The Leyland Society, The Williamson Tunnels, Jonathon Wild and the Willys GP Study Group.

Above: *This photograph was found in the box containing the company's official wartime pictures, but whilst it was not one of their commissions, it was sent by a former Pearson's employee who was in the parade pictured. In his inscription on the back, he wrote he had sent the picture back, because he had painted the Census Number on the truck; Z 5517452, a Truck 15-cwt Half-tracked", from the batch Z5517050-5518172 acquired under S/M 6173 converted to a parade vehicle with others and 'belonged' to the 7th Armoured Division. The date was the 21st July 1945 and the event was the Victory parade in Charlottenburg Chaussee in Berlin. In the back are: Winston Churchill, Field Marshalls Montgomery and Alanbrooke, and Major-General Lewis Lyne, first Military Governor of the British Zone of Berlin and the former GOC 7th Armoured Division.*

THE *The Pearson's of Liverpool Story* SUBSCRIBERS

The persons named on this page have all placed a pre-order subscription to this book, and it is entirely thanks to their kind support that its eventual publication was possible. We regret that only those persons who had confirmed their order by the press date of 5th December 2008 have been included. To those that confirmed subsequent to that date, may we apologise for not being able to include their details at this time. Obviously, subscription editions of strictly limited publications increase their value substantially, and they therefore become a sound investment for the future. If you would like details of how to subscribe to limited edition 'Premier' books from Trans-Pennine/Nostalgia Road, please contact us for advance information.

Paul Agorao
Robert Ainsworth
J. P. Ambler
Nicky Armstrong
Pete Ashby
Peter Aspey
Rolf Sigurd Ask
Maurice Austin
P. V. Bailey
D. R. Ball
Brian Barker
Jordan Baker
Charles George Bates
Brian Baxter
Charles Beckwith
Jean Belzil
Robert Berry
S. M. Birbaum
Eric Blackwell
Malcolm Boegart
Derek Bonfield
Joan Boult
Giel P. Bout
G. P. Bowdley
William Brade
Robert Bragg
G. Britton
Chris Brook
Mr Bullas
Nick Bullock
John M. Burke
Tyson H. Burridge
Mike Cecil
David Chapman
Raymond Chapple
John Chipman
Dennis Chorlton
Maria Clarke
Michael Collins
Paul Corrigan
Thelma Cowdall
S. M. Cuddy
J. D. Cuff
R. Davis
Edward Gavin Delahunty
Sheila Dickson
Cnristian Dominie
G. C. Dray
Ronald Dutton
Alf Edwards
Mr W. E. Ellis
Dennis J. Fleming
John Ford
David Forrest
Leslie Freathy
Dave Froubister
R. G. Gamage
Mike Gammon
P. N. Gannon
Margie Gibney
Alan Godfree
R R Goodey
Mark Graham
Kevin Green
Terence Green
David Griffiths
Robin J. Hannay
Trevor Hanson
George Barry Hartley
David Hayward
Ernest & Sandra Hayward
Graham Hayward
Peter Helm
David Hewson
William Higgins
Mike Hinchey
Bruce Hoad
M. J. B Hogenkamp
John Holmberg
A. J. Hooper
Michael Houlden
A. R. House
John D. Howarth
Geir Iversen
Les Jackson
S. Javis
Dennis Jean
David Johns
A. M. Johnson
Harold Johnston
Mike Keats
Phil Kenny
David Koch
George Kirk
Brian Lamport
Clive Law
Kenneth Lawrence
Dirk Leegwater
Andrew Keith Liddell
George A. C. Little
Mr G. S. Low
Ken Lobley
Javier De Luemlo
J. G. Maddocks
B. A. Martin
Elizabeth Martin
K. Martin
Kevin Martlew
Richard Morris
Brian Morse
Jan Mostek
J. Murden
Jim Murphy
R. W. Mwowczynski
Chris Naylor
Roy Nicholas
Michael Northover
Roy Northover
D. W. Oldbury
M. Ostick
Michael Parker
Doreen Parr nee Trevivian
W. G. Pealing
Alan Pepper
Don Perchard
Mr R. Poole
Alexander Porcelli
Anthony Power
Mr D. Powis
James Purkis
J. Raine
Kevin Reilly
Mark Reynolds
Keith W. Richardson
Matthew Rimmer
Geoff Riseley
Tony Roach
K. J. Roberts
Mr Robertson
A. N. Rogers
Paul Sadler
Anthony Sartorius
Clive Screaton
James Shallow
W. Small
Nigel Stennett-Cox
Barbara Shaw
Matthew Shearer
Anthony Smith
A. M. L Smith
Bob Smith
Douglas Smith
Fred Smith
Jason Smith
Edward Sparks
H. L. Spoelstra
Michael Starmer
David Stevens
Alan Sturge
D Sykes
R. J. Tranner
Edward Tatlock
Chris Taylor
Richard Teesdale
Jeremy Tobin
Leslie Thomas
K P Twell
Hendrik Van Oorspronk
Mandy Veer
M. Vickers
David Vivyan
Dominica Wakelam
Patricia Waller
James Walsh
K. R. Walter
J. R. Walters
Keith Webb
C. Whitehouse
Mr. Whitehouse
Edward Whitworth
Jonathon Wild
Robert Wilson
M. T. Winter
Anne Woodward
William Worthington
John Wynn
Paul Young
Ray Young

This Limited Edition Copy Of

After The War Was Over

is presented to

By The Authors

Alan Earnshaw

David Hayward

Number 453 which is one of only 1,500 produced in Britain